New Daylight

Edited by Naomi Starkey January–April 2010

Suggestions for using *New Daylight*

Find a regular time and place, if possible, where you can read and pray undisturbed. Before you begin, take time to be still and perhaps use the BRF prayer. Then read the Bible passage slowly (try reading it aloud if you find it over-familiar), followed by the comment. You can also use *New Daylight* for group study and discussion, if you prefer.

The prayer or point for reflection can be a starting point for your own meditation and prayer. Many people like to keep a journal to record their thoughts about a Bible passage and items for prayer. In *New Daylight* we also note the Sundays and some special festivals from the Church calendar, to keep in step with the Christian year.

New Daylight and the Bible

New Daylight contributors use a range of Bible versions, and you will find a list of the versions used in each issue at the back of the notes on page 154. You are welcome to use your own preferred version alongside the passage printed in the notes, and this can be particularly helpful if the Bible text has been abridged.

New Daylight affirms that the whole of the Bible is God's revelation to us, and we should read, reflect on and learn from every part of both Old and New Testaments. Usually the printed comment presents a straightforward 'thought for the day', but sometimes it may also raise questions rather than simply providing answers, as we wrestle with some of the more difficult passages of Scripture.

New Daylight *is also available in a deluxe edition (larger format). Check out your local Christian bookshop or contact the BRF office, who can also give more details about a cassette version for the visually impaired. For a Braille edition, contact St John's Guild, 8 St Raphael's Court, Avenue Road, St Albans, AL1 3EH.*

Writers in this issue

David Winter is retired from parish ministry. An honorary Canon of Christ Church, Oxford, he is well known as a writer and broadcaster. His most recent book for BRF is *Pilgrim's Way*.

Steve Aisthorpe lives in Scotland with his wife and two sons. He is a development officer for the Church of Scotland, encouraging mission and discipleship throughout the Highlands and Western Isles. He was previously Executive Director of the International Nepal Fellowship.

Veronica Zundel is an Oxford graduate, writer and journalist. She lives with her husband and son in North London, where they belong to the Mennonite Church.

Naomi Starkey is the Editor of *New Daylight*. She also edits *Quiet Spaces*, BRF's prayer and spirituality journal, as well as commissioning BRF's range of books for adults. She has written *Good Enough Mother* for BRF.

Gordon Giles is a vicar in Enfield, north-west London, previously based at St Paul's Cathedral, where his work involved musical and liturgical responsibilities. He is trained in music, philosophy and theology.

Jennifer Oldroyd worked for many years at the Ashburnham Place conference centre in East Sussex. She was Managing Editor for a major Christian publisher, and in the last few years has had published two books of study material for small groups.

Helen Julian CSF is an Anglican Franciscan sister, currently serving her community as Minister Provincial. She has written *Living the Gospel* and *The Road to Emmaus* for BRF.

Rachel Boulding is Deputy Editor of the *Church Times*. Before this, she was Senior Liturgy Editor at Church House Publishing. She lives in Dorset with her husband and son—and, during school terms, more than 70 teenage boys.

Stephen Cottrell is the Bishop of Reading. He has worked in parishes in London and Chichester, as Missioner in the Wakefield diocese and as part of Springboard, the Archbishop's evangelism team.

Stephen Rand is a writer and speaker who in recent years has shared his time between Jubilee Debt Campaign, persecuted church charity Open Doors and Mainstream, a Baptist church leaders' network. He and his wife Susan live in Oxfordshire, not too far from their grandchildren.

Further BRF reading for this issue

For more in-depth coverage of some of the passages in these Bible reading notes, we recommend the following titles:

978 1 84101 066 3, £8.99

978 1 84101 029 8, £8.99

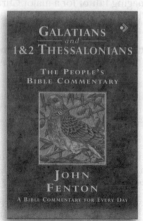

GALATIANS
and
1&2 THESSALONIANS
THE PEOPLE'S
BIBLE COMMENTARY
JOHN
FENTON
A BIBLE COMMENTARY FOR EVERY DAY

978 1 84101 012 0, £7.99

978 1 84101 030 4, £7.99

Naomi Starkey writes...

As I have quite possibly mentioned before, one of the challenges of commissioning Bible reading notes is dealing with the very different types of literature that make up the Bible. While some parts break down neatly into daily reading-sized chunks, other sections (notably prophecy and poetry but also narrative) can be much more difficult to divide up.

In *New Daylight* the Bible passage is limited to around 200 words, so it can be hard to know how best to tackle a story or psalm. The background detail in an Old Testament episode may be fascinating but it means a choice between heavy abridgement of the passage or a somewhat rambling reading from which the contributor may struggle to extract a 'thought for the day'. With psalms, the parallelism of Hebrew poetry (saying the same thing twice in different ways) can result in a reading more repetitive than reflective, unless careful selection is made of key verses.

There is no easy way to deal with this and I sympathise with those readers irritated by rows of '...' on the page. One solution, though, is to make time at some point during the week to read the relevant section of the Bible in full. This is not only for completeness' sake but also to note all the extra comment and detail that go to make up the richness of the text.

In recent issues, I have asked some contributors to focus on a small section of scripture (such as Isaiah 55 and 1 Corinthians 13). The chosen Bible passage can thus be printed in its entirety, but it will be often much shorter than usual. This can encourage us to slow down, to read more meditatively, allowing the words to filter to a deeper level of the heart. Bishop Stephen Cottrell's post-Easter readings from John 20 offer just such an approach in this issue.

Finally, I would like to welcome Steve Aisthorpe to *New Daylight*. I first encountered Steve through reading about his miraculous escape from a potentially fatal climbing accident, an event that was a significant step on his path to faith—and the opening chapter of Brad Lincoln's *Six Men Encountering God* (BRF, 2008). After working abroad with the International Nepal Fellowship, he is now a development officer for the Church of Scotland, encouraging congregations across the Highlands and Western Isles.

The BRF Prayer

Almighty God,

you have taught us that your word is a lamp for our feet and a light for our path. Help us, and all who prayerfully read your word, to deepen our fellowship with each other through your love. And in so doing may we come to know you more fully, love you more truly, and follow more faithfully in the steps of your son Jesus Christ, who lives and reigns with you and the Holy Spirit, one God for evermore. Amen.

Fathers of the faith

Those who don't know where they've come from may well have a problem working out where they're going. Like it or not, we are children of our past, shaped to a large extent by our upbringing, which usually stems from the kinds of examples our parents and grandparents gave us. The same principle operates in the wider Christian Church: however much we may talk of 'new ways of being Church', the truth is that we are part of a tradition of faith going back 2000 years. It might make a good New Year's resolution to determine that in 2010 we shall consciously set out to learn a little bit more about those who followed Christ long ago.

Over the next nine days, we shall visit the earliest days of the Church, not only because the passage that we shall be reading is one of the earliest books of the New Testament but also because we shall be reading it through the eyes of the Christians of the first few centuries, as we will be remembering two great 'Fathers of the faith', Basil the Great and Gregory of Nazianzus. The writer of Hebrews has already reminded his readers of many of the great heroes of faith in our Old Testament. Next, in the passages we shall be reading, he urges them to honour their present leaders and also their parents and teachers, and to remain faithful to what they have taught them.

Basil and Gregory lived in the fourth century. In the previous generation the Emperor Constantine had become a Christian, but the Roman Empire was still largely pagan. Christians were in a minority. Of course, with imperial patronage, the Church had acquired a certain respectability, but at a price. Many had become nominally Christian because it seemed socially advantageous. Perhaps partly for these reasons, the Church was threatened with constant division over both doctrine and discipline and so desperately needed strong, faithful and godly leadership.

As teachers and bishops in the Eastern Church, Basil and Gregory looked more to the new city of Constantinople than to Rome. They lived lives of rigorous personal discipline and fearlessly stood for what they believed to be the apostolic faith. They looked (as Hebrews 13:14 puts it) for 'the city that is to come'. It was that commitment to the priority of the spiritual that enabled them to speak to the world of their time—and to us, today.

David Winter

HEBREWS 12:1–3 (NRSV)

The cloud of witnesses

Therefore, since we are surrounded by so great a cloud of witnesses, let us also lay aside every weight and the sin that clings so closely, and let us run with perseverance the race that is set before us, looking to Jesus the pioneer and perfecter of our faith, who for the sake of the joy that was set before him endured the cross, disregarding its shame, and has taken his seat at the right hand of the throne of God. Consider him who endured such hostility against himself from sinners, so that you may not grow weary or lose heart.

For these readings, we shall use this last part of the letter to the Hebrews to reflect on some of those who, long ago or in our own day, have gone before us on the journey of faith and, by their lives and their vision of God, have provided inspiration for generations of Christians who have followed them. In particular, we shall look tomorrow at the lives of two outstanding Christian leaders—Basil the Great and Gregory of Nazianzus. They lived in a tempestuous time, when the Church was threatened by seductive heresy on the one hand and the dangerous temptation of secular power and influence on the other.

In the phrase from our reading today, they were part of that splendid 'cloud of witnesses' that 'surrounds' the Christians of each generation. They were and are both an example and an inspiration. When many voices and powerful influences distracted believers from 'running the race' of faith, these 'witnesses' kept their eyes firmly on Jesus, the one (as the New Jerusalem Bible puts it) who 'leads us in our faith and brings it to perfection' (v. 2). They defended the faith in the councils of the Church and lived it in their lives. They did not 'grow weary or lose heart' (v. 3). When the true Christian faith had seemed in danger of being blown away by compromise with contemporary culture, they knew where they stood and—more importantly—who it was they followed.

Reflection

Two of the key words in today's passage are endurance and perseverance. If they sound like old-fashioned virtues, that may help to explain why modern Christianity—especially in the Western world—sometimes seems rather flabby and weak-kneed.

DW

Saturday 2 January

HEBREWS 12:4–7 (NRSV)

Strong love

In your struggle against sin you have not yet resisted to the point of shedding your blood. And you have forgotten the exhortation that addresses you as children—'My child, do not regard lightly the discipline of the Lord, or lose heart when you are punished by him; for the Lord disciplines those whom he loves, and chastises every child whom he accepts.' Endure trials for the sake of discipline. God is treating you as children; for what child is there whom a parent does not discipline?

Today the Western Church celebrates the lives of two of the greatest figures of the Eastern Church—Basil the Great and Gregory of Nazianzus. Close friends throughout their lives, from their early days as students at the university of Athens, they were nevertheless quite different characters. Basil was an activist, Gregory a contemplative. At one point their friendship was threatened when Basil accused Gregory of 'slackness' as a bishop!

Both would have known the 'discipline of the Lord' of which our passage speaks. Basil faced ecclesiastical, political and even imperial opposition to his commitment to the apostolic faith; Gregory, a less robust character, faced slander, insults and even physical violence when he set out to reform the church at Constantinople. Eventually this opposition—and his own concern for the good of his flock—cost him his bishopric.

Basil died at the age of 49, worn out by disease and the austerity of his life. He was born into a wealthy and influential family, but, during a time of famine, he had distributed the entire family inheritance to the poor in his city. Gregory was physically weakened throughout his adult life by self-imposed poverty and premature old age. Neither of them felt that other Christians should necessarily imitate their lifestyle. Both men, however, saw such suffering as part of their positive relationship with a Father God who loved them, rather than as something to be avoided at all costs.

Reflection

It's pointless to argue that human life doesn't include suffering, pain and sorrow—we all know that it does—but, for Christians, even these painful things are not pointless or negative. God does not directly cause them, but he does use them—ultimately, for our blessing and the blessing of others.

DW

Sunday 3 January

HEBREWS 12:9–11 (NRSV)

The fruits of discipline

Moreover, we had human parents to discipline us, and we respected them. Should we not be even more willing to be subject to the Father of spirits and live? For they disciplined us for a short time as seemed best to them, but he disciplines us for our good, in order that we may share his holiness. Now, discipline always seems painful rather than pleasant at the time, but later it yields the peaceful fruit of righteousness to those who have been trained by it.

It's strange how 'disciple' and 'discipleship' are perfectly acceptable words for modern Christians, but mention 'discipline' and people start to think of press gangs, punishment and army drills! All three words share the same root, however, and the heart of each is the idea of learning. A disciple is a learner, discipleship is the process of learning and discipline is a means by which we learn.

The early 'Fathers of the faith', like Basil and Gregory, certainly knew about discipline, as we have seen. For them, it was the key to discipleship. Both of them became monks—indeed, for a time, hermits, living a solitary life of prayer and contemplation. While Gregory seems to have retained a longing for this kind of life right through his years as a bishop and pastor, Basil left the solitary life when he was 34 in order to get involved in addressing the pressing needs of the embattled Church of the time.

Needless to say, one doesn't have to become a monk, much less a hermit, to live a disciplined Christian life. As our passage points out, discipline often seems irksome at the time, but, provided the one imposing discipline on us is doing it out of love and we accept it positively, then it will yield the 'peaceful fruit of righteousness'. God's discipline—which sometimes requires of us painful repentance and a willingness to follow his way rather than our own—is essentially the discipline of love. It is not capricious, but works to an agenda of care. The wise Christian welcomes the Lord's discipline, knowing that it works only for our blessing.

Reflection

The disciplined Christian life is, the writer says, a 'training', but, like the discipline of a good and wise parent, it is training that yields fruit, sows peace and promotes what is right and just.

DW

HEBREWS 12:12–16 (NRSV)

The pursuit of peace

Therefore lift your drooping hands and strengthen your weak knees, and make straight paths for your feet, so that what is lame may not be put out of joint, but rather be healed. Pursue peace with everyone, and the holiness without which no one will see the Lord. See to it that no one fails to obtain the grace of God; that no root of bitterness springs up and causes trouble, and through it many become defiled. See to it that no one becomes like Esau, an immoral and godless person, who sold his birthright for a single meal.

This passage sets out the consequences of the disciplined life of faith. From it, the writer suggests, the Christian can gain strength and encouragement—perhaps because it 'straightens the path' by removing perilous bends and pitfalls. It also commits the disciple to the pursuit of peace with everyone, which requires God-given holiness and the eradication of every 'root of bitterness'.

The Fathers of the faith certainly faced these kinds of challenges because the early centuries saw endless controversy within the Church as well as, at times, fierce persecution from outside it. When Gregory faced bitter opposition in Constantinople, where he had struggled to reform the Church, he left voluntarily rather than cause a major disruption, 'for the peace of the church'. To avoid bitterness in circumstances like those is true evidence of grace.

Basil's conflicts were at an even subtler level, but no less destructive. In the fourth century, the Church was in danger of being taken over by the Empire, with the Emperor claiming authority to adjudicate on matters of Christian doctrine and discipline. Basil felt it vital to oppose such ideas and stand for the freedom of the Church to be what the apostles intended it to be, the body of Christ. He was not prepared, in the analogy offered here, to 'sell its birthright' for worldly approval. Like his friend Gregory, however, his life was so transparently Christ-centred that even their opponents could not accuse them of malice or falsehood.

Reflection

Hebrews seems a little tough on Esau! He was angry and bitter at Jacob's deceit, but he was later reconciled with his brother, so the 'root of bitterness' (v. 15) here seems to have been eradicated (see Genesis 33:4).

DW

HEBREWS 12:18–19, 22–24 (NRSV)

A vision of splendour

You have not come to something that can be touched, a blazing fire, and darkness, and gloom, and a tempest, and the sound of a trumpet, and a voice whose words made the hearers beg that not another word be spoken to them... But you have come to Mount Zion and to the city of the living God, the heavenly Jerusalem, and to innumerable angels in festal gathering, and to the assembly of the firstborn who are enrolled in heaven, and to God the judge of all, and to the spirits of the righteous made perfect, and to Jesus, the mediator of a new covenant, and to the sprinkled blood that speaks a better word than the blood of Abel.

Hebrews breathes the atmosphere of the early Church, both in its treatment of the Old Testament and in the spiritual priorities of the writer. The letter is robust and uncompromising, yet deeply Christ-centred. This was very much the tone that Basil, Gregory and other fathers of the faith adopted three centuries later. They too were uncompromising in their personal spiritual discipline, they too set high standards for their flock, they too fought fiercely for the faith handed down. Yet, their eyes were also always on the final goal, the glorious vision of God himself, and on his Son, the source and sustenance of their faith.

So here we have a wonderful picture of that final goal—the heavenly Jerusalem, the glorious city of God. It is thronged with angelic beings in party mood (as we might say). There are the patriarchs of old and there, too, are the 'spirits' of the sanctified 'righteous'. (Does this vision precede the final resurrection and the creation of 'new bodies'?) The writer contrasts this joyful assembly with the fearful people who approached Mount Sinai for the giving of the Law. Those gathering at the heavenly Mount Zion have been 'sprinkled' in the blood of Christ, the guarantee of their acceptance under the new covenant. They come boldly, 'in full assurance of faith' (10:19–22). Theirs is not presumption but assurance, based on God's promise. This distinction is important!

Reflection

Abel's blood for vengeance
Pleaded to the skies,
But the blood of Jesus
For our pardon cries.

Trans. Edward Caswall (1814–78)

DW

HEBREWS 13:1–4 (NRSV)

Angels unawares

Let mutual love continue. Do not neglect to show hospitality to strangers, for by doing that some have entertained angels without knowing it. Remember those who are in prison, as though you were in prison with them; those who are being tortured, as though you yourselves were being tortured. Let marriage be held in honour by all, and let the marriage bed be kept undefiled; for God will judge fornicators and adulterers.

Although these words were addressed to the church in first-century society, they have a timeless quality. Indeed, they may seem particularly relevant to our Western world today. The most attractive feature of the Church has always been what the writer calls 'mutual love', the shared warmth, care and loving concern that marks Christian fellowship at its best. Recently I sat behind a woman in our church whose husband had died suddenly two days earlier and was moved to see how many people simply came up to touch her on the shoulder or squeeze her hand or put an arm around her—usually without a word—as we waited for the service to start. Many of us have experienced the healing power of such 'mutual love'.

Many, too, will have been blessed by Christian hospitality. Society in apostolic times was very familiar with the duty of hospitality, but here we are thinking of spontaneous and generous welcome. Abraham and Sarah offered such hospitality to three strangers who turned out to be 'angels' (Genesis 18:1–15). It could, the writer suggests, happen to us!

In those early centuries of the faith, many Christians were put in prison and some were tortured. Their fellow believers were to identify with them in their sufferings—the true meaning of 'sympathy'. The reference to marital fidelity probably reflects the challenge presented to Christians by widespread sexual laxity in such places as Corinth. The believers were not to be corrupted by what was going on around them and new converts would have been expected to aspire to the highest standards of fidelity. A word for today, indeed!

Reflection

Mutual love will always welcome the stranger, care for the suffering and treat human relationships with loyalty and respect.

DW

Thursday 7 January

Hebrews 13:5–8 (NRSV)

Honouring our leaders

> Keep your lives free from the love of money, and be content with what you have; for he has said, 'I will never leave you or forsake you.' So we can say with confidence, 'The Lord is my helper; I will not be afraid. What can anyone do to me?' Remember your leaders, those who spoke the word of God to you; consider the outcome of their way of life, and imitate their faith. Jesus Christ is the same yesterday and today and for ever.

Paul congratulated the Christians at Thessalonica because they had become 'imitators of us' (Paul, Sylvanus and Timothy) 'and of the Lord' (1 Thessalonians 1:6), as though they were one and the same thing. In one sense they were and, ideally, it should always be true that those who are leaders in the Church are also examples of the Christlike life for the disciples. Although we recognise that leaders sometimes fall short of that high standard, many of us would want to honour particular people who have been influential in shaping our faith.

The real thrust of this passage, however, concerns the quality of life expected of all Christians, leaders or (as we all are) followers. Paul describes love of money as a 'root of all kinds of evil' (1 Timothy 6:10), so it should be shunned and contentment—that most elusive virtue—should take its place. As we have seen in the lives of those who have been examples to us, whatever difficulties we face, 'the Lord is my helper' (v. 6). In him we can have total confidence because, unlike even the finest of our earthly leaders, he is the same 'yesterday and today and for ever' (v. 8). To be 'in Christ' is to be embedded in the eternal changelessness of God himself.

'Remember your leaders' (v. 7). We should hold in our hearts the lessons they taught us, the inspiration of their lives, the imprint of their characters. I can think of many people down the years who have profoundly shaped my faith and to remember them is to be reminded to keep closely to the path on which they set me. Perhaps also this was a call to remember their leaders in prayer. Sadly, sometimes we are quicker to criticise our leaders than we are to pray for them.

Reflection

We may have many leaders, but only one master, who is their master, too.

DW

Friday 8 January

HEBREWS 13:12–17 (NRSV)

The eternal city

Therefore Jesus also suffered outside the city gate in order to sanctify the people by his own blood. Let us then go to him outside the camp and bear the abuse he endured. For here we have no lasting city, but we are looking for the city that is to come. Through him, then, let us continually offer a sacrifice of praise to God, that is, the fruit of lips that confess his name. Do not neglect to do good and to share what you have, for such sacrifices are pleasing to God. Obey your leaders and submit to them, for they are keeping watch over your souls and will give an account. Let them do this with joy and not with sighing—for that would be harmful to you.

The early Church seems to have had a deeper awareness than Christians today of the priority of the eternal. Although they often lived in cities surrounded by strong walls and dominated by splendid buildings, they knew how fragile life was, how vulnerable to disease, famine and disaster. They looked for 'the city that is to come' (v. 14) for true security. They knew what we tend to forget, that the strongest walls and cleverest human plans are in the end subject to decay.

This does not mean, the writer argues, that we should detach ourselves from the needs and problems of the world around us. It simply means that we should see them through different eyes. Like Jesus, who died 'outside the city gate' (v. 12)—in the place of vulnerability and insecurity—we are called to leave our ivory towers of secure faith and go where the action is—to stand with those in need, share sacrificially with those who suffer and offer ourselves in loving service to God and to the world. Anyone who has read the lives of the saints and martyrs of those early centuries will know that this is not empty talk. The fathers (and mothers) of the faith—the leaders who kept watch over their people's souls—walked the talk and lived the life.

Reflection

'So heavenly minded they're no earthly use'—that's the complaint sometimes made about Christians. The fact is that to be truly 'heavenly minded' is to be the greatest possible use: just think of Martin Luther King, Mother Teresa and Desmond Tutu!

DW

Saturday 9 January

HEBREWS 13:20–21 (NRSV)

Made complete

Now may the God of peace, who brought back from the dead our Lord Jesus, the great shepherd of the sheep, by the blood of the eternal covenant, make you complete in everything good so that you may do his will, working among us that which is pleasing in his sight, through Jesus Christ, to whom be the glory for ever and ever. Amen

The letter to the Hebrews ends with this marvellous blessing, a widely used and greatly loved prayer. It brings together several of the book's themes and breathes the essential spirituality of the early Church. It invokes the 'God of peace', a phrase used by Paul in a passage where he also speaks of the 'peace of God' (Philippians 4:7, 9). The latter is a gift of God; the former is an attribute of his divine nature. Just as God is love, so he is peace, and those who belong to him can dwell in his peace.

The blessing speaks of the work of God in sanctification—the process by which he turns sinners into saints. This is brought about, says the prayer, through the blood shed by the 'great shepherd of the sheep', the Lord Jesus. Through his sacrifice we are forgiven; through his resurrection, we are given new life. All of this makes for a 'complete' salvation—one that affects every part of the believer's life. This is not simply a private faith, but one that enables us to do the will of God, to achieve what is 'pleasing in his sight'. Nothing could better describe the total Christian life—a life that is complete, tuned to the purpose of God, confident of the Saviour's forgiveness, responsive to the needs of those who will be blessed by the good and loving action to which we are called.

This prayer almost certainly comes from the very earliest days of the Church. It displays the faith for which generations have been prepared to sacrifice time, fortune, worldly power and even life itself. It is, as this prayer demonstrates, a life-changing faith. In the fourth century it changed the lives of men like Basil and Gregory. Down the centuries it has changed the lives of countless men and women and, today, a very different world, it is still doing so.

Reflection

May the God of peace make us complete in everything good.

DW

John 3:22—5:40

The tension mounts. Shouts from the crowd reach a crescendo. Then all eyes turn to the digital clock: '3... 2... 1...' There is an eruption of ecstatic shouts: 'Happy New Year!' It happens every year, yet thousands flood into London's Trafalgar Square and town squares around the world to experience the anticipation and euphoria of the beginning of a new year.

Within John's Gospel, there is the ultimate countdown. It is not related to an annual occurrence, but to a once-in-eternity, never-to-be-repeated event. John, writing some years after the events themselves, lets us in on the mystery early on (John 1:14), but to those present at the time, the identity of a remarkable man became clear gradually—revealed sign by miraculous sign, claim by claim.

More than other Gospel writers, John explains how the miracles of Jesus were more than actions in history: they provide windows into the character of God and the identity of Jesus. Having just miraculously fed thousands, Jesus revealed himself to be the 'bread of life' (6:48); while healing a blind man, Jesus claimed to be 'the light of the world' (9:5); Jesus' encounter with the Samaritan woman at Jacob's well (4:29) revealed God's omniscience, his perfect knowledge and Jesus' intimate relationship with his Father.

If the signs were amazing, then Jesus' claims were outrageous. The significance of his early activities was made clear by his claim: 'My Father is always at his work to this very day, and I, too, am working' (5:17). This statement, made on a sabbath, fuelled the rage of his critics, who 'tried all the harder to kill him' (5:18). What could they do with this man? Not only was he breaking the sabbath but he was even calling God his own Father.

As the signs and the claims stack up in the course of the Gospel, the clock ticks, the countdown continues. We see that Jesus is fully aware of the eternal plan in which he plays his role centre stage: to his mother at the wedding in Cana he says, 'My time has not yet come' (2:4); seven times we are told, 'a time is coming'; his persecutors could not touch him because 'his time had not yet come' (7:30); as the time approaches for him to die and rise and consummate the hope for all generations, he prays, 'Father, the time has come' (17:1).

Three... two... one... All is about to be revealed.

Steve Aisthorpe

Sunday 10 January

John 3:22–26 (NIV)

Competition or cause for rejoicing?

After this, Jesus and his disciples went out into the Judean countryside, where he spent some time with them, and baptised. Now John also was baptising at Aenon near Salim, because there was plenty of water, and people were constantly coming to be baptised. (This was before John was put in prison.) An argument developed between some of John's disciples and a certain Jew over the matter of ceremonial washing. They came to John and said to him, 'Rabbi, that man who was with you on the other side of the Jordan—the one you testified about—well, he is baptising, and everyone is going to him.'

The music quickens. The secret agent glances over his shoulder, a face in the crowd comes into focus and we know that he is being followed. Our journey of following Jesus is often characterised by just the opposite: an uncanny sense that someone has gone *before* us.

Jesus, too, had that experience of someone going ahead of him. He walked into communities prepared by John's ground-breaking ministry. Like an Olympic cyclist slipstreaming his teammate before pulling out of the pack, revealing his brilliance and racing to victory, Jesus steps out of obscurity and presses forward as John fades into the background.

Those with eyes to see will discover the footprints of God along the daily path. Rather than blazing a new trail, we are walking in his steps. What is fresh and challenging for us is part of what he has 'prepared in advance' (Ephesians 2:10). How sad, then, when signs that should encourage us become the basis for comparison and competition. Arguments about doctrine are often thin disguises for envy. The dispute between John's disciples and 'a certain Jew' (John 3:25) began as a religious one, but soon revealed itself as jealousy and a misunderstanding of God's purposes.

When we find ourselves confused or envious, we do well to follow the example of John's disciples. They went to their master, who understood the bigger picture. Our master, too, will reveal glimpses of his plans (15:15).

Prayer

Father, please anoint my eyes so that I can see the ways in which you have gone ahead of me. Where I see your purposes advancing, help me to rejoice as you rejoice.

SA

JOHN 3:27–30 (NIV)

Knowing me, knowing you

To this John replied, 'A person can receive only what is given from heaven. You yourselves can testify that I said, "I am not the Christ but am sent ahead of him." The bride belongs to the bridegroom. The friend who attends the bridegroom waits and listens for him, and is full of joy when he hears the bridegroom's voice. That joy is mine, and it is now complete. He must become greater; I must become less.'

John the Baptist, seeing the potential for rivalry taking root between his disciples and those of Jesus, seeks to diffuse the situation by citing a profound spiritual truth: 'A man can receive only what is given him from heaven' (v. 27). It is a maxim that Jesus himself reinforced in his words to Pilate: 'You would have no power over me if it were not given to you from above' (19:11). The central purpose of John's Gospel—to help people believe in Jesus (20:31)—is well served by John the Baptist here. Both Johns share the same burning desire: for people to know who Jesus is.

John the Baptist finds his identity in relation to the identity of Jesus. He is best man to the groom. At a Jewish wedding the best man, or *Shoshben*, had a unique role in bringing the bride and groom together. His final task was to guard the bridal chamber until, in the dark, he heard and recognised the groom's voice. Once the bride and groom were safely together, his task was complete. John's task was to bring the bride, Israel, to her groom, Jesus. Now he could rejoice. That the influence of Jesus should increase and their own diminish led to fear among John's disciples, but John's heart overflowed with joy and a sense of 'mission accomplished'.

We too find our true identity as we discover more of Jesus' identity and our relationship to him. Knowing ourselves and knowing Jesus are not only linked but inextricably intertwined. In the words of theologian and reformer John Calvin (*The Institutes of the Christian Religion*, 1599), 'There is no deep knowing of God without the deep knowing of self, and no knowing of self without deep knowing of God.'

Prayer

Lord, as I turn to you, may I discover fresh insights into your character and a greater awareness of who I am in you. Amen

SA

JOHN 3:31–36 (NIV)

Choices, choices

[John said] 'The one who comes from above is above all; the one who is from the earth belongs to the earth, and speaks as one from the earth. The one who comes from heaven is above all. He testifies to what he has seen and heard, but no one accepts his testimony. The person who has accepted it has certified that God is truthful. For the one whom God has sent speaks the words of God, for God gives the Spirit without limit. The Father loves the Son and has placed everything in his hands. Those who believe in the Son have eternal life, but those who reject the Son will not see life, for God's wrath remains on them.'

So many choices each day—some trivial ('Hmm, the blue socks or the red ones?'); some substantial ('How to spend my life, where, with whom…?'), some with eternal consequences.

Today, the one who is above all (v. 31), the one sent by God (v. 34), the one to whom the Spirit is given without measure (v. 34) and in whose hands are all things (v. 35) offers us a choice. Grace is free, but how we respond is our choice.

Jesus does not present us with a smorgasbord of options. There are two choices—no third way, no middle road, no reasonable compromise. His words echo the solemn life-or-death choices that were set before the people of Israel: 'See I set before you today life and prosperity, death and destruction… Now choose' (Deuteronomy 30:15, 19); 'choose for yourselves this day whom you will serve' (Joshua 24:15).

The wrath of God (John 3:36) is an unpopular and uncomfortable notion, but the Bible clearly states that our loving Father is also the holy God who cannot remain indifferent to evil—justice must be done. For all who choose well, it has been done and there is no condemnation (Romans 8:1–4). The eternal life we are offered is free, but only because the giver himself, out of his unfathomable love, paid the highest price imaginable (John 3:16).

Reflection

'Now choose life, so that you and your children may live and that you may love the Lord your God, listen to his voice, and hold fast to him. For the Lord is your life' (Deuteronomy 30:19–20).

SA

Wednesday 13 January

JOHN 4:5–9 (NIV)

Danger! Automatic barriers

So [Jesus] came to a town in Samaria called Sychar, near the plot of ground Jacob had given to his son Joseph. Jacob's well was there, and Jesus, tired as he was from the journey, sat down by the well. It was about the sixth hour. When a Samaritan woman came to draw water, Jesus said to her, 'Will you give me a drink?' (His disciples had gone into town to buy food.) The Samaritan woman said to him, 'You are a Jew and I am a Samaritan woman. How can you ask me for a drink?' (For Jews do not associate with Samaritans.)

I once helped a friend who ran a pig farm. The pigs were enclosed by a single-strand electric fence that was barely visible, but delivered a painful jolt when touched. When the time came to move the pigs and part of the fence was removed, it was almost impossible to persuade them to cross the imaginary line where the fence had been. Experience had taught them not to go there.

The world Jesus knew was criss-crossed by powerful, invisible barriers—religious, ethnic and gender barriers for starters. The feud between Jews and Samaritans had been festering for centuries. Racial rivalry, religious disputes and ethnic cleansing had contributed to a toxic state of affairs.

Rabbis said that to eat the bread of a Samaritan was tantamount to eating the flesh of a pig, the most denigrating act imaginable. To be a Samaritan was bad enough, but a Samaritan *woman*? Even worse! Some rabbis were forbidden to greet a woman in public, even their own wife or daughter.

Being so distant, culturally and in time, we struggle to grasp the radical nature of Jesus' encounter at Jacob's well. Not only was he conversing with a Samaritan and a woman at that, but someone who, because of her shameful history (v. 18), needed to fetch water when others would not, in the intense glare and heat of midday—a daily walk of shame.

Throughout the Gospels we find Jesus treating barriers with indifference. He sees beyond stereotypes and prejudice—right through to the person, created in the divine image; fallen, yes, but dearly loved.

Prayer

Gracious Father, anoint my eyes, so that I can see people as you do. Give me the courage to follow you through all barriers and love the 'unlovable'.

SA

Thursday 14 January

John 4:10–15 (NIV)

Water—but not as we know it

Jesus answered her, 'If you knew the gift of God and who it is that asks you for a drink, you would have asked him and he would have given you living water.' 'Sir,' the woman said, 'you have nothing to draw with and the well is deep. Where can you get this living water? Are you greater than our father Jacob, who gave us the well and drank from it himself, as did also his sons and his flocks and herds?' Jesus answered, 'All who drink this water will be thirsty again, but those who drink the water I give them will never thirst. Indeed, the water I give them will become in them a spring of water welling up to eternal life.' The woman said to him, 'Sir, give me this water so that I won't get thirsty and have to keep coming here to draw water.'

Jesus was tapping into a rich seam of prophetic thought here. When the word of the Lord came to Jeremiah, he said, 'My people have committed two sins: They have forsaken me, the spring of living water' (Jeremiah 2:13). Isaiah caught a glimpse of the coming Messiah as he called out, 'Come, all you who are thirsty, come to the waters' (Isaiah 55:1). Zechariah saw a day coming when 'a fountain will be opened to the house of David and the inhabitants of Jerusalem, to cleanse them from sin and impurity' (Zechariah 13:1).

Once again, John is eager that we know just who Jesus is. For those with ears to hear, Jesus is saying, 'You're waiting for the coming Christ? It's me!'

Malcolm Muggeridge (1906–1990), after reflecting on a life in journalism and television—a life of considerable fame and material success—had this to say: 'Yet I say to you, and I beg of you to believe me, multiply these tiny triumphs by a million, add them all together, and they are nothing—less than nothing, a positive impediment—measured against one draught of that living water Christ offers to the spiritually thirsty, irrespective of who or what they are' (quoted in J. Gladstone, *Living with Style*, Welch, 1986).

Reflection

'Come, receive'—not stagnant water, but living water; not a temporary fix, but an ever-flowing fountain; not because of your exemplary life, but because of your genuine longing.

SA

Friday 15 January

John 4:16–24 (NIV)

Incisive words, healing words

[Jesus] told her, 'Go, call your husband and come back.' 'I have no husband,' she replied. Jesus said to her, 'You are right when you say you have no husband. The fact is, you have had five husbands, and the man you now have is not your husband. What you have just said is quite true.' 'Sir,' the woman said, 'I can see that you are a prophet. Our ancestors worshipped on this mountain, but you Jews claim that the place where we must worship is in Jerusalem.' Jesus declared, 'Believe me, woman, a time is coming when you will worship the Father neither on this mountain nor in Jerusalem. You Samaritans worship what you do not know; we worship what we do know, for salvation is from the Jews. Yet a time is coming and has now come when the true worshippers will worship the Father in spirit and in truth, for they are the kind of worshippers the Father seeks. God is spirit, and his worshippers must worship in spirit and in truth.'

Like a scalpel in the hands of a master surgeon, the words of Jesus work incisively and pare away the pretence. Suddenly the verbal jousting is over and the woman sees herself as never before. How could she have ever imagined that a little economy with the truth would cover her shame? Yet Jesus' intention is not just to expose falsehood, but also bring truth.

Shocked by what she sees—herself, exposed and ashamed—her thoughts turn to God. How and where can she make the necessary sacrifice? Religious rivalries have left her perplexed. Jesus cuts through the confusion and points out that 'a time is coming and has now come' (v. 23), long anticipated by the prophets, when the nations will worship 'every one in its own land' (Zephaniah 2:11) and the Lord will be worshipped in every place (Malachi 1:11).

There is a temple from which true worship springs. It is a holy place—made holy by the Spirit of truth: 'Don't you know that you yourselves are God's temple and that God's Spirit lives in you?' (1 Corinthians 3:16).

Reflection

Prophecy has been called criticism based on hope. Jesus strips away the cloak of self-deception but also institutes a life lived in truth and loving relationships, one cleansed, shaped and empowered by the Spirit.

SA

JOHN 4:28–30, 39–42 (NIV)

Gossiping the gospel

Then, leaving her water jar, the woman went back to the town and said to the people, 'Come, see a man who told me everything I ever did. Could this be the Christ?' They came out of the town and made their way towards him… Many of the Samaritans from that town believed in him because of the woman's testimony, 'He told me everything I ever did.' So when the Samaritans came to him, they urged him to stay with them, and he stayed two days. And because of his words many more became believers. They said to the woman, 'We no longer believe just because of what you said; now we have heard for ourselves, and we know that this man really is the Saviour of the world.'

Shocked and dumbfounded, the disciples look at one another, then at the abandoned water jar. The deserted jar—a touching detail in John's eye-witness account—speaks of the woman's passionate desire to share her story with her neighbours. The shame that had driven her to avoid those same neighbours by visiting the outlying well in the full heat of the day had gone. What a contrast between the shamefaced stumble to the well and the hasty return home. Of course, it may be that the jar was not forgotten at all, as there was absolutely no doubt that she would be back soon enough!

We each have our own stories of our encounters with Christ. Some are amazing; others, we may think, are lacking in any kind of drama except as far as we are concerned. Whether extraordinary or low-key, however, our stories are powerful. The Spirit takes such experiences and uses them, like the Samaritan woman's tale, to draw people to Jesus.

The townsfolk of Sychar were soon flocking to meet Jesus. If the woman's story had been compelling, the words of the master himself were clearly overwhelming. The long-excluded and looked-down-on were drawn into the circle of God's grace. If they, the resented and detested, were included, then there could be no limit, no barrier too high. This was truly the 'Saviour of the world' (v. 42).

Prayer

Heavenly Father, please increase my desire to tell of your wonderful grace, provision, guidance and power. Use my story, lived and spoken, to draw many closer to you. Amen

SA

Sunday 17 January

JOHN 4:31–38 (NIV)

Mission possible

Meanwhile [Jesus'] disciples urged him, 'Rabbi, eat something.' But he said to them, 'I have food to eat that you know nothing about.' Then his disciples said to each other, 'Could someone have brought him food?' 'My food,' said Jesus, 'is to do the will of him who sent me and to finish his work. Do you not say, "Four months more and then the harvest"? I tell you, open your eyes and look at the fields! They are ripe for harvest. Even now those who reap draw their wages, even now they harvest the crop for eternal life, so that the sower and the reaper may be glad together. Thus the saying "One sows and another reaps" is true. I sent you to reap what you have not worked for. Others have done the hard work, and you have reaped the benefits of their labour.'

I once climbed the notorious north face of the Eiger in the Swiss Alps with some others. We climbed for three days, sleeping on icy ledges, yet we barely ate. Climbing the Eiger had been a dream since my youth. We were fuelled not primarily by food, but by our passion.

Jesus was exhausted, yet when the disciples brought food he was not interested. What did he mean by 'food you know nothing about'? When Jesus drove traders from the temple, the disciples remembered Psalm 69: 'Zeal for your house will consume me' (John 2:17), but they had not understood that this zeal, this passion to do the will of his Father, governed everything he did. All else was secondary; nothing else mattered.

John's Gospel tells us about Jesus being 'sent' by God 44 times. From the Latin word for 'a sending', *missio*, we get the word 'mission'. Jesus was supremely aware that he was a man on a mission. He had a divine purpose with eternal consequences.

The disciples could see the swaying fields of corn for which this area was renowned, but Jesus pleaded, 'open your eyes' (4:35). He was seeing the harvest of Samaritan lives taking place right in front of them—and the bigger harvest of which this was a foretaste. The last thing on his mind was food.

Reflection

'As the Father has sent me, I am sending you' (20:21). What parallels does Jesus have in mind between his own sense of being 'sent' and ours?

SA

John 4:46–53 (NIV)

From tiny seeds to mighty oaks

Once more [Jesus] visited Cana in Galilee, where he had turned the water into wine. And there was a certain royal official whose son lay sick at Capernaum. When this man heard that Jesus had arrived in Galilee from Judea, he went to him and begged him to come and heal his son, who was close to death. 'Unless you people see miraculous signs and wonders,' Jesus told him, 'you will never believe.' The royal official said, 'Sir, come down before my child dies.' Jesus replied, 'You may go. Your son will live.' The man took Jesus at his word and departed. While he was still on the way, his servants met him with the news that his boy was living. When he enquired as to the time when his son got better, they said to him, 'The fever left him yesterday at the seventh hour.' Then the father realised that this was the exact time at which Jesus had said to him, 'Your son will live.' So he and all his household believed.

I met Chandra in a hospital in Nepal. He had been cured of leprosy, but the disease had ravaged his body. His face remains with me—distorted, yet radiant. It was his words, though, that brought tears to my eyes: 'I'm so grateful for my leprosy. Otherwise I might never have heard about Jesus.'

The illness that afflicted the royal official's son took his father on a round trip of 40 miles. Judging by his pleading with Jesus, he, like most parents, would have gone to the ends of the earth if it had meant that his child would have been saved. In his wisdom and love, Jesus led him on a faith-growing journey.

That the physical journey began at all shows the presence of seeds of faith (you can almost see the headline: 'Royal Official Travels to Plead with Galilean Carpenter'), but Jesus wanted to grow and stretch that infant faith. Did the official think that he needed to go to Capernaum? Was he believing or just desperate? That the official 'took Jesus at his word' (v. 50) is no small thing. It was seven in the evening—too late to travel, so confirming the outcome would be delayed. Departing without Jesus meant that it was all or nothing.

Reflection

Faith matures through testing (James 1:3–4). Dare you pray for more faith?

SA

Tuesday 19 January

JOHN 5:2–9 (NIV)

Do you want to be changed?

Now there is in Jerusalem near the Sheep Gate a pool, which in Aramaic is called Bethesda and which is surrounded by five covered colonnades. Here a great number of disabled people used to lie—the blind, the lame, the paralysed. One who was there had been an invalid for thirty-eight years. When Jesus saw him lying there and learned that he had been in this condition for a long time, he asked him, 'Do you want to get well?' 'Sir,' the invalid replied, 'I have no one to help me into the pool when the water is stirred. While I am trying to get in, someone else goes down ahead of me.' Then Jesus said to him, 'Get up! Pick up your mat and walk.' At once the man was cured; he picked up his mat and walked.

Having spent time in some of the poorer quarters of Asia I can assure you that Jesus' question, 'Do you want to get well?' is not as strange as it seems. Begging is a long-term livelihood for many around the world and a visible disability—the more dramatic the better—can be an income-enhancing asset.

The man at the pool had been unable to walk for 38 years. Yes, 38 years! During that time he would have developed strategies and a lifestyle to fit his abilities and limitations. The implications of those limitations being radically changed were immense. It is to this man's great credit that, despite a cautious initial response, he accepted the healing that Jesus was offering.

What about us? Jesus' question, 'Do you want to get well?' is a penetrating one, whatever our physical condition. Once we accept Jesus' call 'Follow me', staying the same is not an option. God's ultimate purpose for us is that we will 'be conformed to the likeness of his Son' (Romans 8:29). That means healing and change, being prepared to cooperate with Jesus as he invites us out of what is familiar and comfortable. Change is a defining characteristic of life in general and at the very heart of a life following Jesus.

Prayer

Father, thank you that, in your grace, you meet me where I am, but also that your love is too great to leave me there. Show me what it means today for me to follow you and to grow into greater Christlikeness. Amen

SA

Wednesday 20 January

JOHN 5:9–10, 16–17 (NIV)

24/7 and legalism

At once the man was cured; he picked up his mat and walked. The day on which this took place was a Sabbath, and so the Jews said to the man who had been healed, 'It is the Sabbath; the law forbids you to carry your mat.'... So, because Jesus was doing these things on the Sabbath, the Jews persecuted him. Jesus said to them, 'My Father is always at his work to this very day, and I, too, am working.'

The busiest times in our town centre are the early hours of Saturday and Sunday. On the edge of town, the supermarket car park is never empty. In an age of '24/7' it is difficult for us to comprehend the strength of feeling of Jesus' contemporaries regarding the sabbath.

Surely all who saw the healed paralytic walking should have rejoiced? Indeed, those who knew their scripture might have wondered if this was the promised Christ. After all, when the Messiah came, the lame would 'leap like a deer' (Isaiah 35:6); he would 'strengthen the feeble hands [and] steady the knees that gave way' (v. 3).

To understand the hatred stirred up by Jesus' compassionate healing, we need to understand the atmosphere of the day: 'The law of the sabbatical rest was perhaps the most important of all the bulwarks by which Judaism was protected from erosion by the encompassing paganism' (L. Newbigin, *The Light has Come*, Handsel Press, 1982).

The sabbath was intended as something beautiful, a day of rest and refocusing, but it had descended into legalistic small-mindedness, with 39 classifications of activity to avoid, including 'carrying a burden'. While intended to prevent the sabbath from becoming indistinguishable from any other day, the rules reached ever-greater extremes of pettiness. If the man carrying his bed had been a furniture remover, his critics may have had a point, but their comments really demonstrated a misguided rigour that emphasised the word of the law over the spirit of the law.

Jesus did not refute the sabbath. The sabbath principle was clearly demonstrated in the rhythms of his life (Luke 5:16; Mark 6:31), but he did refuse to allow compassion to be limited by trivialmindedness.

Reflection

How do we avoid the excesses of contemporary '24/7' and legalism—and embrace and enjoy the sabbath as God intends?

SA

JOHN 5:19–22 (NIV)

Like Father, like Son

[Jesus said] 'I tell you the truth, the Son can do nothing by himself; he can do only what he sees his Father doing, because whatever the Father does the Son also does. For the Father loves the Son and shows him all he does. Yes, to your amazement he will show him even greater things than these. For just as the Father raises the dead and gives them life, even so the Son gives life to whom he is pleased to give it. Moreover, the Father judges no one, but has entrusted all judgment to the Son.'

In 1934, two post office engineers, F.G. Balcombe and J.A. Sheppard, were determined to push back the boundaries of cave exploration and so they devised a rudimentary system for diving through submerged passages. It involved a long hosepipe, through which air was fed to the diver by means of a modified bicycle pump. A basic telephone connection allowed communication through the icy cold, inky waters. There can be few more potent images of total dependence: one partner pioneering uncharted territory, the other supplying air, encouragement and guidance through the rubber umbilical cord.

When Jesus topped his healing on the sabbath with an implication of parity with God (v. 17), it is difficult to imagine the outrage that would have caused. Yet, his claims became even more astonishing: the giving of life and judging of humanity, clearly attributes of God, he claimed as part of his remit. Then, as Jesus spoke of a relationship with the Father so close as to make him equal with God, the rage and indignation escalated.

Jesus, God in flesh, reveals God to us in the best way that our frail minds can understand. 'He is the image of the invisible God' (Colossians 1:15). He also showed what it means to be fully human. We were created to live in intimate relationship and utter dependence on our creator Father. By becoming human, Jesus took on the limitations that implied (Philippians 2:6–8), but still lived in wholehearted, love-inspired obedience to his Father. He longs for those of us who call him 'Lord' to aspire to ever-greater depths of devotion and new heights of reverential reliance.

Reflection

Jesus invites us to live as he did: 'Remain in me… apart from me you can do nothing' (John 15:4–5).

SA

Friday 22 January

JOHN 5:24–27 (NIV)

Plain truth and authentic hope

[Jesus said] 'I tell you the truth, those who hear my word and believe him who sent me have eternal life and will not be condemned; they have crossed over from death to life. I tell you the truth, a time is coming and has now come when the dead will hear the voice of the Son of God and those who hear will live. For as the Father has life in himself, so he has granted the Son to have life in himself. And he has given him authority to judge because he is the Son of Man.'

How many legs does a dog have if you call the tail a leg? Four; calling a tail a leg doesn't make it a leg. These words, attributed to Abraham Lincoln, are entertaining and refreshing because truth has become a slippery commodity. The online encyclopedia Wikipedia says that, 'The term truth has no definition about which a majority of philosophers and scholars agree'.

The phrase 'I tell you the truth' (vv. 24, 25) recurs throughout John's Gospel. Jesus is 'full of... truth' (see 1:14); he is 'the truth' (John 14:6). Our culture is one of hyperreality—filled with false celebrity and relative truth—and Jesus' words are cool water in a parched land. When we are drowning in the counterfeit, Jesus does not just throw us a rope, he comes to us and his teaching brings freedom to those who hear and obey (8:32).

Another oft-repeated phrase of Jesus' is expanded and enriched here. Not only is 'a time coming', but it 'has now come'. Eternal life has come—*and* is yet to come. We therefore celebrate a current truth and yet yearn for the fulfilment of our hope.

We have stepped from death to life. That is a present reality (Ephesians 2:1–5), but our own deficiencies, the brokenness of lives around us and daily reminders of our race's disposition to exploit and spoil fuel a profound longing for the kingdom's consummation (Romans 8:19). A heart cry of the Early Church was 'Maranatha'—'Come, O Lord!' (1 Corinthians 16:22).

Reflection

'May the God of hope fill you with all joy and peace as you trust in him, so that you may overflow with hope by the power of the Holy Spirit' (Romans 15:13). May the God of truth grant us courage for lives of radical authenticity.

SA

Saturday 23 January

JOHN 5:36–40 (NIV)

Your ID please!

[Jesus said] 'I have testimony weightier than that of John. For the very work that the Father has given me to finish, and which I am doing, testifies that the Father has sent me. And the Father who sent me has himself testified concerning me. You have never heard his voice nor seen his form, nor does his word dwell in you, for you do not believe the one he sent. You diligently study the scriptures because you think that by them you possess eternal life. These are the scriptures that testify about me, yet you refuse to come to me to have life.'

Returning to the UK after more than a decade living in Asia, I struggled to gather the evidence I needed to prove my identity. An old-style driving licence and a passport issued in a small Asian embassy didn't cut the mustard and, in order to get trustworthy ID, it seemed that I needed trustworthy ID already!

In the passages we have been reading, Jesus has been raising hackles and provoking big questions. The biggest question was regarding his ID. Could this carpenter's son from Galilee really be who he seemed to be claiming to be? Where were his credentials?

Jesus insists that nobody should blindly accept his witness about himself (v. 31). The rigorous test of authenticity demanded by the scriptures—that of multiple witnesses (Deuteronomy 19:15)—should be applied.

So John carefully assembles the witnesses. There is the witness of John the Baptist (John 5:33–35) and the work given to him by God that he is doing (v. 36). Another key witness is the very scriptures that the people have been 'diligently' studying (vv. 39–40). How could people who had meticulously examined the scriptures miss the promised Messiah? Had they been reading to prove their beliefs rather than test them? Had they thought that such knowledge was a virtue in itself that earned God's favour?

Jesus is clear: the scriptures do indeed establish his true ID, but, ultimately, they are not a doorway to salvation, but, rather, a signpost to him, who alone offers salvation.

Reflection

In our diligent reading of scripture, let's not miss the point: 'These scriptures are all about me! And here I am, standing right before you' (John 5:40, THE MESSAGE).

SA

A letter to Asia Minor: Galatians

We do not know when Paul's letter to the Galatians was written, nor precisely which area of Asia Minor it was sent to. It is in a standard letter format of the time: a 'rebuke/request' letter, in which the writer points out a way in which the recipient has offended the writer, then asks for a change of behaviour.

In every other letter from Paul, the apostle introduces himself and then goes on to give thanks for the recipients and their faith. This one, by contrast, goes straight into a rebuke: 'I am astonished that you are so quickly deserting the one who called you' (Galatians 1:6). This is a letter by someone who is really upset, which you can tell from his passionate tone.

Traditionally, following Martin Luther's commentary, Galatians has been regarded as a letter telling us that it is faith, not works, which makes us children of God. Luther's interpretation, however, reflects his concerns and those of others who read him, rather than this being Paul's original emphasis.

More recently, scholars have written about Galatians in terms of it giving a new perspective on Paul. They suggest that the main focus of the letter is the influence of maverick Christian teachers who have been saying that, in order to follow Christ, it is necessary to become a Jew and keep the Jewish Law. This also affects our readings of Romans, a letter that covers similar ground at more length and in greater depth.

Even Paul's opening greeting, 'Grace to you and peace'—a combination of a Greek and a Hebrew salutation—sets the tone for the theme, which is that the distinction between Jews and Gentiles is now abolished.

If this angle is valid, how can Galatians be relevant to us in the 21st century? While our church situation is very different, we too can easily fall into thinking that our discipleship is all about keeping certain rules or having a certain cultural identity. Like the Galatians, we know that we are saved by grace through faith, but that doesn't stop us from trying to be sanctified by sticking to lists of commandments.

In contrast, Paul tells us in 5:25, 'If we live by the Spirit, let us also be guided by the Spirit' or, in some translations, 'walk in' or 'keep in step with' the Spirit. We need this message just as much as the Galatians did.

Veronica Zundel

Sunday 24 January

GALATIANS 1:1–8 (NRSV, ABRIDGED)

Here is the news

Paul an apostle—sent neither by human commission nor from human authorities, but through Jesus Christ and God the Father... To the churches of Galatia: Grace to you and peace from God our Father and the Lord Jesus Christ, who gave himself for our sins to set us free from the present evil age... I am astonished that you are so quickly deserting the one who called you in the grace of Christ and are turning to a different gospel—not that there is another gospel, but there are some who are confusing you and want to pervert the gospel of Christ. But even if we or an angel from heaven should proclaim to you a gospel contrary to what we proclaimed to you, let that one be accursed!

I wonder when you last switched on the TV or radio (or browsed the Internet) and heard unalloyed good news? In a world ravaged by war, climate chaos and economic depression, we rarely look forward to the news bulletins. I'm writing this just before Barack Obama's inauguration as US President. Millions are looking to him to be good news for the world, but no doubt, by the time you read this, he will already have been criticised.

Right at the start of his letter to churches in Asia Minor, Paul establishes its two themes: his own authenticity as an apostle and the centrality of Christ to the world's salvation. Both are key to his gospel being what its name means: good news.

Paul asserts that his calling comes not from the established Church, but direct from God. He wishes grace and peace in the name of Christ, 'who gave himself for our sins to set us free' (v. 3). This is not Christ the teacher, the healer or the prophet, though all these roles are important—this is Christ the redeemer, who rescues us from all the power-mongering and oppression of a fallen world.

The Galatians seem to think that they have found good news in a place where it isn't to be found. They have listened with too much trust to unreliable voices, which can only lead to their ruin. We, too, need to listen critically and discern which 'good news' is truly good.

Reflection

In a world of many opinions, which voices do you trust most?

VZ

GALATIANS 1:13–17 (NRSV)

I was a teenage moralist

You have heard, no doubt, of my earlier life in Judaism. I was violently persecuting the church of God and was trying to destroy it. I advanced in Judaism beyond many among my people of the same age, for I was far more zealous for the traditions of my ancestors. But when God, who had set me apart before I was born and called me through his grace, was pleased to reveal his Son to me, so that I might proclaim him among the Gentiles, I did not confer with any human being, nor did I go up to Jerusalem to those who were already apostles before me, but I went away at once into Arabia, and afterwards I returned to Damascus.

In my youth as a Christian (and I'm not sure things have changed much), a 'good testimony' was one that related a scandalous past from which the speaker had been redeemed. Those of us who were converted from a fairly respectable life might have felt that our stories were worth very little in comparison.

Paul launches here into a long and complex account of his life and conversion. It's not for the purpose of giving his audience a vicarious thrill with tales of sex and crime. Indeed, his story is that of a 'good boy' in all respects: not only a devout Jew but also one who travelled far and wide to root out heresy. If he had been a communist, he would have been a party official who consigned dissidents to imprisonment and torture.

The point here is to show the Galatians how useless Paul's pious past is when it is compared to the wholeness Jesus brings. The Galatians are beginning to believe that keeping Jewish law will help them follow Christ. Paul demonstrates that, in his own life, it produced a man whose mission in life was to condemn others.

We need to be careful not to dismiss Judaism as purely a legalistic faith. The Old Testament is shot through with words of grace and forgiveness: if it wasn't, would we still read it today? Paul, too, is not dismissing Judaism; rather, he is saying, if you have tasted the wine of the new covenant, why would you want to return to the old?

Reflection

'God… set me apart before I was born and called me' (v. 15). Do you have a sense of God's call in your life? What is God calling you to?

VZ

GALATIANS 2:1, 3, 7, 9–10 (NRSV)

No extras

Then after fourteen years I went up again to Jerusalem with Barnabas, taking Titus along with me... But even Titus, who was with me, was not compelled to be circumcised, though he was a Greek... On the contrary, when [the Church leaders] saw that I had been entrusted with the gospel for the uncircumcised, just as Peter had been entrusted with the gospel for the circumcised... and when James and Cephas and John, who were acknowledged pillars, recognised the grace that had been given to me, they gave to Barnabas and me the right hand of fellowship, agreeing that we should go to the Gentiles and they to the circumcised. They asked only one thing, that we remember the poor, which was actually what I was eager to do.

Have you ever played the game where a message is whispered around a circle of people, getting comically distorted, so that 'Send reinforcements, we're going to advance' famously becomes 'Send three and fourpence, we're going to a dance'?

The Galatians seem to think that this is what has happened to Paul's message on its way from Jerusalem to Galatia. Knowing that the Jerusalem church still keeps the Jewish law, they believe that Paul has left out this vital part of Christian discipleship. It's to counter this that Paul insists (as we saw yesterday) that he didn't get his gospel from the Jerusalem church, but direct from God.

Today he is addressing another part of the misunderstanding. Although he did not get his message second hand from Jerusalem, it has in fact been ratified by the Jerusalem church. Indeed, he has been affirmed by the leaders in his specialist ministry to the Gentiles.

So there are no 'hidden extras' that Paul ought to be telling the Gentiles about the realities of being a Christian. All they need is belief in Christ and the gift of the Spirit. Sadly, many churches today still make unwarranted extra requirements of disciples.

I find it interesting that the one request the Jerusalem church does make of Paul is nothing to do with doctrine: it is that he collect for the poor. Do we give similar priority to social action today?

Reflection

'Whoever would approach [God] must believe that he exists and that he rewards those who seek him' (Hebrews 11:6). That's all.

VZ

Galatians 2:11–14 (NRSV)

Separate tables?

But when Cephas came to Antioch, I opposed him to his face, because he stood self-condemned; for until certain people came from James, he used to eat with the Gentiles. But after they came, he drew back and kept himself separate for fear of the circumcision faction. And the other Jews joined him in this hypocrisy, so that even Barnabas was led astray by their hypocrisy. But when I saw that they were not acting consistently with the truth of the gospel, I said to Cephas before them all, 'If you, though a Jew, live like a Gentile and not like a Jew, how can you compel the Gentiles to live like Jews?'

'No meeting together without eating together.' I've heard of a church that has this policy. 'Table fellowship' has always been central to a thriving Christian community.

In the key Jerusalem conference described in Acts 15, the Church decides that the only restrictions it will place on Gentile Christians are those which safeguard the ability of Jews and Gentiles to eat together (v. 29). There was a time, however, when Peter (Cephas) drew back from eating with Gentile believers. Perhaps he was influenced by other Jewish believers within the Church or wanted to be well thought of among Jews in general. Unfortunately, others—even Paul's friend Barnabas—joined him in this rejection of what Peter had been told by God in a vision: that no food is unclean (Acts 11:1–12).

From the very beginning, there was a danger that the Church, composed of Jews and Gentiles together, would split into those two groups. It was for this reason that Greek-speaking deacons were chosen to care for Greek-speaking widows (Acts 6:1–6). Eventually, the Church 'solved' this problem by parting company entirely with its Jewish roots—causing great loss.

Countless wars and conflicts around the world have been caused by ethnic differences, but, to quote Jesus in a different context, 'it will not be so among you' (Matthew 20:26). Sadly, even in our own times, churches have been divided in this way.

Paul is insistent that all ethnic communities are equal within the Church and anything else is a travesty of the gospel.

Prayer

Pray for countries experiencing ethnic conflicts, especially for the Christians living there.

VZ

GALATIANS 2:15–16, 19–20 (NRSV)

Holier than thou?

We ourselves are Jews by birth and not Gentile sinners; yet we know that a person is justified not by the works of the law but through faith in Jesus Christ. And we have come to believe in Christ Jesus, so that we might be justified by faith in Christ, and not by doing the works of the law... For through the law I died to the law, so that I might live to God. I have been crucified with Christ; and it is no longer I who live, but it is Christ who lives in me.

Just as John Wesley famously felt his heart 'strangely warmed' by Luther's commentary on Romans, so John Bunyan was deeply inspired by Luther's words on Galatians. Passages like today's have long been used to teach the concept of 'justification by faith' rediscovered by Luther.

From the previously mentioned new perspective on Paul, however, scholars have questioned whether this is the best interpretation of such passages. They suggest that Paul is not actually putting a wedge between 'works religion' and faith—an idea that has sometimes been used to divert the Church from social action.

Instead, Paul is continuing with his argument that the Jewish believers have no right to regard themselves as more Christian than the Gentile believers. On the contrary, not even faithful Jews can justify themselves before God by religious practices—it is only by faith in Christ that we become disciples.

So the opposition here is not between 'faith and works' in general, but between those who still think that their status as Jews makes them the true people of God and those who know that a new people of God has been founded, composed of all peoples and nations.

This might seem irrelevant to us, who are mainly Gentiles (though there are still Jews like myself who have come to Christ), but the overarching principle continues to apply: there is nothing in nationality, status, education, experience or Christian doctrine that makes one group of people more Christian than another. We may be better or worse followers of Jesus, but everyone who follows Jesus is among the redeemed people of God.

Reflection

'It is no longer I who live, but it is Christ who lives in me' (v. 20). What difference does this make to your everyday life?

VZ

Friday 29 January

GALATIANS 3:1–8 (NRSV, ABRIDGED)

It's all in the Spirit

You foolish Galatians! Who has bewitched you?... Did you receive the Spirit by doing the works of the law or by believing what you heard? Are you so foolish? Having started with the Spirit, are you now ending with the flesh? Did you experience so much for nothing?... Just as Abraham 'believed God, and it was reckoned to him as righteousness', so, you see, those who believe are the descendants of Abraham. And the scripture, foreseeing that God would justify the Gentiles by faith, declared the gospel beforehand to Abraham, saying, 'All the Gentiles shall be blessed in you.'

When I was a student, I kept meeting people who asked me, 'Have you been baptised in the Spirit?' I didn't understand, but later I had an overwhelming spiritual experience that lit everything up in my life as a Christian.

On biblical grounds, though, I don't see Christian conversion as a 'two-stage' experience, with water baptism first, followed by a filling with the Spirit. In the process of conversion, as we meet it in most of Acts and here in Galatians, we are baptised in the name of the Father, Son and Holy Spirit and new Christians are expected to see the Spirit at work in their lives.

Paul here reminds the Galatians of all that they have received as a result of their conversion: the Spirit is within and among them, doing wondrous things and changing them into the image of Christ.

Christian discipleship is often portrayed as following a set of rules that tell us the correct Christian attitude on everything from abortion to Zen. We are by no means free of the mistake the Galatians made: thinking that we are saved by the Spirit but sanctified by the law. Most of us don't eat kosher or celebrate Jewish festivals, but we all have our own little series of hurdles that new Christians have to jump to be fully part of the Church.

Paul recalls us to Abraham, father of all who follow the one God. He points out that God's relationship with Abraham predates Abraham's circumcision, which is only an outward sign of an inward reality. The Spirit is not summoned up by ritual practices: he blows where he wills (John 3:7–8).

Prayer

Thank God for giving you the Holy Spirit and ask for the Spirit to work in you.

VZ

GALATIANS 3:19–24 (NRSV, ABRIDGED)

Law—what for?

Why then the law? It was added because of transgressions, until the offspring would come to whom the promise had been made... Is the law then opposed to the promises of God? Certainly not! For if a law had been given that could make alive, then righteousness would indeed come through the law. But the scripture has imprisoned all things under the power of sin, so that what was promised through faith in Jesus Christ might be given to those who believe. Now before faith came, we were imprisoned and guarded under the law until faith would be revealed. Therefore the law was our disciplinarian until Christ came, so that we might be justified by faith.

In schools nowadays, pupils struggling with the curriculum or, indeed, particularly gifted pupils can be assigned a mentor to help them overcome barriers to learning. All pupils also have a form tutor who looks after their welfare in school. These are the nearest modern equivalents I can find to the 'disciplinarian' Paul talks about here. His job (normally with a well-off family) was to escort the pupil to and from school and discipline the child so that the teacher could devote himself to teaching.

Quite understandably, the Galatians are asking (or Paul expects them to ask) what the point of the Jewish law is if it can't actually transform human life. Paul turns to two metaphors: the law as jailer and the law as disciplinarian. In a sense, he is telling us that the law existed to create favourable conditions for the Jewish people to encounter God. It both highlighted the fact that humans are inherently sinful and provided a vision of what the just society would look like, if only we could attain it.

You could also say that the law is like the ploughman who turns over the soil, exposing all the stones and rubbish that need to be removed. The law prepares the ground for the new life that springs up in Christ.

As Jesus says to the Samaritan woman, 'salvation is from the Jews' (John 4:22). We owe a great deal to Christianity's Jewish roots and the Church can go wrong when it forgets that.

Reflection

'Charity begins at home', but doesn't have to end there. Equally, salvation is from the Jews, but doesn't stop with them.

VZ

GALATIANS 3:25–29; 4:6–7 (NRSV)

Time bombs

But now that faith has come, we are no longer subject to a disciplinarian, for in Christ Jesus you are all children of God through faith. As many of you as were baptised into Christ have clothed yourselves with Christ. There is no longer Jew or Greek, there is no longer slave or free, there is no longer male and female; for all of you are one in Christ Jesus. And if you belong to Christ, then you are Abraham's offspring, heirs according to the promise... And because you are children, God has sent the Spirit of his Son into our hearts, crying, 'Abba! Father!' So you are no longer a slave but a child, and if a child then also an heir, through God.

Many years ago I heard a speaker talk on Galatians 3:28: 'There is no longer Jew or Greek... slave or free... male and female.' Paul, he suggested, planted three time bombs with these words. The first bomb went off almost at once, abolishing the distinction between Jew and Gentile. The second took over 1800 years to go off, with the campaign against slavery. The third is going off in our own time, as we rediscover the equality of male and female in Christ.

Later, I noticed something else about this verse. Baptism, unlike circumcision, is a sign that is not confined to men. By its very nature, it does away with a fundamental religious divide between the sexes.

Baptism is not a magic rite that automatically makes us Christian, however. It is our faith, not being baptised in itself, that enables us to be 'born from above' (John 3:3) as children of God.

Nearly 90 years ago, my mother, born Jewish, was adopted by a childless Jewish couple. Although she knows who both her birth parents were, she regards her adoptive parents as her 'real' parents—the ones who 'rescued' and raised her. In a sentence I've missed out for length (Galatians 4:5), Paul says Jesus came 'so that we might receive adoption as children'. In other words, just being Jewish—or, for that matter, growing up in a 'Christian country'—does not make us children of God. Belonging to Jesus does.

Prayer

'To all who received him, who believed in his name, he gave power to become children of God' (John 1:12). Thank God for adopting you.

VZ

Monday 1 February

GALATIANS 4:21–26, 31—5:1 (NRSV, ABRIDGED)

Foremothers

Tell me, you who desire to be subject to the law, will you not listen to the law? For it is written that Abraham had two sons, one by a slave woman and the other by a free woman... Now this is an allegory: these women are two covenants... Hagar is Mount Sinai in Arabia and corresponds to the present Jerusalem, for she is in slavery with her children. But the other woman corresponds to the Jerusalem above; she is free, and she is our mother... So then, friends, we are children, not of the slave but of the free woman. For freedom Christ has set us free. Stand firm, therefore, and do not submit again to a yoke of slavery.

In the 1970s and 1980s, Christian women (including myself) began to notice that they were not often included in the stories we tell each other about our faith. Sunday school materials and sermons would tell of Abraham, Moses, David and Solomon as our spiritual forefathers, but were strangely silent on Deborah, Ruth, Esther or the Hebrew midwives of Exodus 1:15. So we began to write commentaries, liturgies, prayers that noticed the women of God and explore the many stories of women in the Bible with a fresh eye.

Today's reading was a particular revelation and encouragement when I discovered it. Paul has been talking about Abraham as the father of our faith, but at this point he turns to a story of two women—the slave girl forced to bear a child for her master and the free woman to whom the promise of a son was made. Rather than dwelling on the tangled motives of Abraham, Sarah and Hagar, he uses the two women as a picture of the difference between sticking to the traditions of Judaism and our freedom in Christ.

It must have been quite a shock for Jewish readers to find that they had been 'in slavery'. Perhaps even today, 'For freedom Christ has set us free' (Galatians 5:1) is not a message we are always ready to hear. We prefer to have our lives tidily regulated by a set of dos and don'ts, but, Paul says, 'we are children... of the free woman' (4:31) and we should beware of any leader or teacher who tries to bind us with new sets of rules.

Prayer

Teach me, Lord, what freedom in Christ means.

VZ

GALATIANS 5:2, 6, 13–14 (NRSV)

Faith works

Listen! I, Paul, am telling you that if you let yourselves be circumcised, Christ will be of no benefit to you… For in Christ Jesus neither circumcision nor uncircumcision counts for anything; the only thing that counts is faith working through love… For you were called to freedom, brothers and sisters; only do not use your freedom as an opportunity for self-indulgence, but through love become slaves to one another. For the whole law is summed up in a single commandment, 'You shall love your neighbour as yourself.'

A writer friend of mine, hearing that I was writing these notes, was inspired to go and read Galatians herself for the first time. 'Seems to me,' she e-mailed, 'he's saying faith in Christ Jesus is the point, circumcision is not the point… it doesn't matter whether you're circumcised or not.' That seemed to me a very fair summary from someone who has not been brought up with the traditional view that Paul is writing about faith versus works.

It also seems to me that Paul has by now said just about all he wants to say about circumcision and Jewish practice. He wants to move on to weightier matters. The key verse is the second half of verse 6: 'the only thing that counts is faith working through love'. In other words, there is no opposition between faith and works, because good deeds are the natural outcome of faith or, as James rather sardonically put it, 'Show me your faith without works, and I by my works will show you my faith' (James 2:18).

About 25 years ago, I won a national award for my columns in *Christian Woman* magazine. The trophy was a stone sculpture of an open hand holding an apple. As I travelled home on the underground train, carrying this rather heavy ornament, I thought that I would just look up again the Bible passage I had read that morning, to remind me of what it was. I had to laugh when I found it was John 15:16: 'I appointed you to go and bear fruit'!

We have been grafted into the true vine (John 15:5) for a purpose: to bear fruit. Our freedom in Christ is freedom to live a Christlike life.

Prayer

Holy gardener, help me to endure pruning and produce healthy fruit.

VZ

Wednesday 3 February

GALATIANS 5:16–21 (NRSV)

Thorns in the flesh

Live by the Spirit, I say, and do not gratify the desires of the flesh. For what the flesh desires is opposed to the Spirit, and what the Spirit desires is opposed to the flesh; for these are opposed to each other, to prevent you from doing what you want. But if you are led by the Spirit, you are not subject to the law. Now the works of the flesh are obvious: fornication, impurity, licentiousness, idolatry, sorcery, enmities, strife, jealousy, anger, quarrels, dissensions, factions, envy, drunkenness, carousing, and things like these. I am warning you, as I warned you before: those who do such things will not inherit the kingdom of God.

I'm not a betting woman, but I think that I could safely bet that most of you don't have these problems in your church: fornication, impurity, licentiousness, idolatry, sorcery, drunkenness, carousing. Such blatant sins are liable to get people thrown out of churches (though I'm not so sure about idolatry, which takes many and insidious forms, including idolising past traditions!).

Wait a minute, though; do you have any of the following in your church: enmities, strife, jealousy, anger, quarrels, dissensions, faction, envy? These are the sins of 'respectable' people and they creep insidiously into all of us. We had better look to the plank in our own eye, rather than the speck in our neighbour's (see Matthew 7:3–5), when it comes to such impulses.

What does the opposition between 'flesh' and 'Spirit' mean? It doesn't mean that we should ignore our physical body and its needs. Rather, 'the flesh' is everything in us that undermines our good intentions: our self-centredness, our tacit acceptance of the devious ways of the world, our lust for power over others. These are the tendencies that rule-based religion cannot touch, for they are deep-seated and only the power of the Holy Spirit can overcome them.

We are right to make laws against racism, sexism, corruption and so on, but no law, religious or secular—can root out human sin.

Similarly, 'living by the Spirit' is not achieved simply by making resolutions.

Reflection

'You can't make people nicer by punishing them', I heard a radio presenter say.

VZ

GALATIANS 5:22–25 (NRSV)

Goodness gracious

By contrast, the fruit of the Spirit is love, joy, peace, patience, kindness, generosity, faithfulness, gentleness, and self-control. There is no law against such things. And those who belong to Christ Jesus have crucified the flesh with its passions and desires. If we live by the Spirit, let us also be guided by the Spirit.

When criticised for an innocent action, people are apt to say in self-defence, 'There's no law against it.' I'm rather amused by Paul's remark, surely meant to be a little joke, that there's no law against love, joy, peace, patience and all the other fruit of the Spirit in his inspiring list.

How does fruit grow? Certainly not by the gardener standing in front of the tree and commanding it to 'Grow, grow!' A fruiting branch must be firmly attached to the trunk, so that nutrients and water can flow up to it from the earth. It may also have to be pruned (as we saw in John 15) to get rid of twigs that are taking the tree's strength but not producing any fruits. Pruning is the gardener's job, though; we are not authorised to declare our fellow believers unfruitful and try to get rid of them!

You could write a whole book about each one of the qualities Paul lists (hey, that's rather a good idea—maybe I should have a go). They cover inward feelings, outward attitudes and actions towards others. If everyone had them, we would have a very different society.

While Paul is not putting a wedge between faith and works, he is putting a wedge between the 'works' of the flesh, and the 'fruit' of the Spirit. Unkind, unloving, ungentle acts and attitudes are produced from the selfish thoughts we have inside as, 'out of the abundance of the heart the mouth speaks' (Matthew 12:34). We don't need any help from demons or other outside influence to make us do wrong, but kindness, generosity and self-control are not works but fruit: the outworkings of the inner transformation that God's Spirit is effecting in our hearts.

Who are the people you most admire? I'm ready to guess that they're people who have these virtues.

Prayer

Choose one aspect of the fruit of the Spirit and ask God to nurture it in you.

VZ

GALATIANS 6:1–5 (NRSV)

Loving the sinner

My friends, if anyone is detected in a transgression, you who have received the Spirit should restore such a one in a spirit of gentleness. Take care that you yourselves are not tempted. Bear one another's burdens, and in this way you will fulfil the law of Christ. For if those who are nothing think they are something, they deceive themselves. All must test their own work; then that work, rather than their neighbour's work, will become a cause for pride. For all must carry their own loads.

My church tradition, the Mennonites, has sadly been only too good at detecting others' transgressions and dealing with them without a lot of gentleness. 'The ban' or 'shunning', based on Matthew 18:15–17, was originally a non-violent alternative to what the state churches did, which was to torture and kill those who went astray. Over the centuries, however, it became a way of making the church feel pure by excluding others.

Perhaps you have seen the film *Chocolat*, where the young priest preaches his first extempore sermon, not written for him by the mayor. He asks if the church might not do better to define itself by whom it includes, rather than what and whom it excludes. When I hear talk of 'the exclusive claims of Christ' I always want to add 'the inclusive call of Christ'.

So Paul's recommendation for the treatment of sin in the church is aimed towards restoration, not exclusion. We have already heard that 'gentleness' is a fruit of the Spirit. Here Paul asserts that not only must our discipleship be 'in the Spirit' but our discipline of each other must be also.

Now what about 'bear one another's burdens' and 'all must carry their own loads'? Is this a contradiction? Paul is using two different Greek words: by 'burdens' he probably means the trials and sorrows of life as well as the burden of sin, while by 'loads' he means the responsibilities we have in Christ. We must judge our own achievements by our calling, not by comparison with others.

We are allowed to be proud of things we have done well. What we are not allowed is to think that they make us superior to others.

Reflection

What do you think is meant by 'the law of Christ'?

VZ

Saturday 6 February

GALATIANS 6:11–18 (NRSV, ABRIDGED)

Re-creation

See what large letters I make when I am writing in my own hand! It is those who want to make a good showing in the flesh that try to compel you to be circumcised... they want you to be circumcised so that they may boast about your flesh. May I never boast of anything except the cross of our Lord Jesus Christ, by which the world has been crucified to me, and I to the world. For neither circumcision nor uncircumcision is anything; but a new creation is everything!... From now on, let no one make trouble for me; for I carry the marks of Jesus branded on my body. May the grace of our Lord Jesus Christ be with your spirit, brothers and sisters. Amen.

Have you ever overheard ministers comparing the size of their congregations? It seems that even we Christians like to boast about our spiritual or evangelistic achievements.

Writing his conclusion to his letter, Paul expresses his suspicion of the 'circumcision faction', questioning their motives for requiring believers to keep the Jewish law. In contrast to their focus on religious practice, he focuses on the cross of Christ. By identifying in our baptism with Christ's death and resurrection, we have become 'a new creation'. It's not just people who are being renewed, but also the whole of creation is being restored to what it was meant to be (see Romans 8:20–21).

The opening verse here, and references elsewhere in Galatians (4:15), have been taken to mean that Paul suffered from eye disease. If so, the restoration of all creation would have meant a lot to him, as it does to everyone who struggles with disability, mental health difficulties or pain in relationships.

Right at the end of the letter, he returns to his own credentials as an apostle—just to make sure that they will listen! Some have taken the statement about 'the marks of Christ' to mean that Paul had the 'stigmata', spontaneous wounds on his body matching the wounds of Jesus. It is more likely that he is talking about his injuries from floggings and other forms of persecution. He is, in other words, speaking from experience.

Prayer

Use the final sentence of today's reading as a prayer for any friend who needs to feel the grace of God in their spirit.

VZ

Covenant people in Exodus 20—34

We resume our readings in Exodus after the section dealing with the Ten Commandments (covered in *New Daylight* last May). This section is a relatively large amount of Bible text to cover in two weeks, so I have adopted a 'highlights' approach. It is worth reading the rest of each chapter as well, however, if only to appreciate the astonishing amount of detail in God's plans for the tabernacle, the altars and the rest of his requirements for establishing the worshipping life of Israel.

Having said that, I do not have space to provide much background information, but I will focus—as is the aim of *New Daylight*—on drawing out a helpful 'thought for the day'. Of course there is a huge amount to be said about ancient Middle Eastern culture, religious practices and so on and, as a starting point for further exploration, I suggest the People's Bible Commentary volume on Exodus by Hugh R. Page Jr (BRF, 2006) and Alan Coles' volume in the Tyndale Old Testament Commentaries series (1973, 2008).

In preparing these readings, I was struck by how the stakes could hardly be higher. On the one hand, God is setting out exactly how the people of his covenant nation are to worship him and atone for their sins, yet, on the other, Moses has to plead with God to spare the people after an appalling act of betrayal and rebellion.

What I also noticed is the contrast between the most holy God—who must be approached with due ceremony and reverence—and the intimate relationship that Moses enjoyed with him. This intimacy is summarised at the end of Deuteronomy (34:10): 'No prophet has risen since in Israel like Moses, whom God knew face to face'. As people of the new covenant, instituted by Jesus, we are familiar with the idea of 'Father God' and it is salutary to be reminded of God's utter holiness. In the light of his blazing splendour, our poverty of spirit and threadbare excuses are shown up for what they are.

Thank God, then, that he is both infinitely holy and also infinitely forgiving. Thank God, too, that through Jesus he has told us that 'Blessed are the poor in spirit' (Matthew 5:3). If we come to him humbly, pretending nothing, offering everything, he will make us, like the Israelites long ago, true children of Abraham, heirs of all that he has promised.

Naomi Starkey

Sunday 7 February

Exodus 20:18–21 (TNIV)

God in the darkness

When the people saw the thunder and lightning and heard the trumpet and saw the mountain in smoke, they trembled with fear. They stayed at a distance and said to Moses, 'Speak to us yourself and we will listen. But do not let God speak to us or we will die.' Moses said to the people, 'Do not be afraid. God has come to test you, so that the fear of God will be with you, to keep you from sinning.' The people remained at a distance, while Moses approached the thick darkness where God was.

We should remember that the 'trumpet' here means the *shofar*, the ram's horn, used in worship and also to mark moments of great significance in the life of God's people. The word translated as 'lightning' in the passage can mean 'torch' or 'flame' and is used in Genesis 15:17 to describe the sign of God's presence ('a smoking firepot and a flaming torch').

We should not envisage some kind of firework display with orchestral accompaniment, but a terrifying, teeth-chattering event. It sounds like a volcanic eruption, but there are no volcanoes (extinct or otherwise) on the Sinai Peninsula. This is the presence of God—a theophany, to use the technical term.

Surprisingly, Moses tells the people not to be afraid. This seems contradictory when he explains that God has come to test them so that 'the fear of God' keeps them from sinning. How can they 'fear God' and yet not be afraid? In fact, to 'fear' God in this context means to honour and respect him, not to be afraid of him. This is the sense of Proverbs 1:7, for example, where we read: 'The fear of the Lord is the beginning of knowledge' (NRSV).

For many people today, having a nodding acquaintance with the Church can be no more than a cheap insurance policy against the risk of an after-life or a handy way of identifying themselves as cultured, community-minded citizens. God is not a lifestyle choice, however, a mix-and-match brand that we can adapt to suit our personal preference. Yes, he is love, as revealed through his Son, but he is also the Lord Almighty, creator of the cosmos, maker of 'all things visible and invisible', as the Nicene Creed reminds us.

Reflection

Dare we, like Moses, enter the 'thick darkness where God is'?

NS

Exodus 20:22–24; 21:1 (TNIV)

Laws for the covenant people

Then the Lord said to Moses, 'Tell the Israelites this: "You have seen for yourselves that I have spoken to you from heaven: do not make any gods to be alongside me; do not make for yourselves gods of silver or gods of gold. Make an altar of earth for me and sacrifice on it your burnt offerings and fellowship offerings, your sheep and goats and your cattle. Wherever I cause my name to be honoured, I will come to you and bless you…" These are the laws you are to set before them.'

These verses introduce a section of laws—first, a list of dos and don'ts, then a series of examples illustrating various legal principles, covering a range of issues from the ownership of Hebrew servants to sabbath-keeping and instructions about three annual festivals.

This covenant nation must be different from those around them. Their community life must be of the very highest standard, because they are God's people, the visible standard by which God will be perceived and judged by the watching world. Accordingly, they are to value all human life, even the most vulnerable. They must show respect for possessions, animate or inanimate; they must respect the land and not exhaust its richness.

It is tempting to view this mass of legality as limiting, even crippling, but, as Hugh Page puts it, the law was a 'living tradition whose energy emanated from the Lord and gave life to all who sought to follow its precepts' (*PBC Exodus*, p. 102). He continues, 'by agreeing to obey the laws of God, the Hebrews made themselves a holy people', just as under the new covenant Christians are given eternal life and made holy by accepting Jesus as their Saviour and being baptised.

Note that here God speaks 'from heaven', not 'from the mountain'. God chose Sinai to make his revelation, but he was not the 'god of the mountain'. We should also note the simplicity of the altar (contrasting with the elaborate structures we shall read about later). This altar could be made and used as needed, because the people could worship God in more than one place. He would bless them with his coming at the time of his choosing.

Reflection

Churches are not in themselves holy; it is the coming of God's Spirit that hallows a place.

NS

Exodus 23:20–21, 31–33 (TNIV, abridged)

Promised land

'See, I am sending an angel ahead of you... to bring you to the place I have prepared. Pay attention to him and listen to what he says. Do not rebel against him; he will not forgive your rebellion, since my Name is in him... I will establish your borders from the Red Sea to the Mediterranean Sea, and from the desert to the River Euphrates. I will give into your hands the people who live in the land, and you will drive them out before you. Do not make a covenant with them or with their gods. Do not let them live in your land or they will cause you to sin against me, because the worship of their gods will certainly be a snare to you.'

This section (vv. 20–33) concludes the terms of God's covenant. It is similar in style to Deuteronomy, combining blessings, curses and exhortations. This approach was common for political treaties of the time, as was the concluding admonition about not making covenant with anybody else, whether human or divine.

What may well strike us most powerfully is the description of the covenant land—and what would happen to those already living there. Knowing the still troubled history of this part of the world, can we really still accept this passage as 'the word of the Lord'?

My view is this: the passage (and others like it) describes what God called his people to do at a particular time. They were not to form alliances with the locals because that risked ceasing to be distinctive, God's holy nation—which is what happened. They began to worship the local gods and the land was eventually lost in the catastrophe of exile, although the hope of a new beginning remained.

When Jesus came, though, he was not like the expected messiah—a military hero restoring to Israel its ancient boundaries. He came to open the way for people to live as children of the Father, fulfilling the purposes of the original covenant. The challenge to us is whether or not we accept the terms of his new covenant—repent, believe, be baptised—that he holds out to the whole world.

Reflection

'For to us a child is born... And he will be called Wonderful Counsellor, Mighty God, Everlasting Father, Prince of Peace' (Isaiah 9:6, NIV).

NS

EXODUS 24:9–12, 15–16 (TNIV)

Seeing God

Moses and Aaron, Nadab and Abihu, and the seventy elders of Israel went up and saw the God of Israel. Under his feet was something like a pavement made of lapis lazuli, as bright blue as the sky. But God did not raise his hand against these leaders of the Israelites; they saw God, and they ate and drank. The Lord said to Moses, 'Come up to me on the mountain and stay here, and I will give you the tablets of stone with the law and commandments I have written for their instruction.'... When Moses went up on the mountain, the cloud covered it, and the glory of the Lord settled on Mount Sinai.

In chapter 24, the covenant is finally ratified, with the sacrificial blood of young bulls (vv. 4–6). Moses reads out the Book of the Covenant (v. 7) and the people promise to obey, having heard the promises and warnings. When things begin to unravel later, they can't say he hadn't warned them!

The breathtaking episode described here may be less familiar to us than the visions of Isaiah and Ezekiel at the start of their prophetic ministries and the moment when Moses famously saw God from behind (33:23). This episode sounds almost casual, as if one of those elders came down and told his wife, 'Yeah, we went up the mountain, saw God, had lunch...'

Who knows exactly what they saw? The sense of beauty and brightness resonates with similar moments in scripture (Ezekiel 1:16 and Revelation 4:3–6) and the implication is that they received a revelation of glory but also mercy. They did not shrivel away in the radiance of God's presence but instead shared a covenant feast, sealing the promises made on both sides.

What happened to them after such an experience? Sadly, in Leviticus 10, we read that Nadab and Abihu, both sons of Aaron, were struck dead after offering 'unauthorised fire before the Lord, contrary to his command' (v. 1, NIV). Despite (or perhaps because of) glimpsing God's glory, they had seemingly forgotten the rightful 'fear' or awe that is the foundation of wisdom.

Reflection

They went up the mountain in response to God's summons (Exodus 24:12). Are we ever so busy that we fail to hear his call and miss the moment when he reveals himself?

NS

EXODUS 25:1–9 (TNIV, ABRIDGED)

The beauty of holiness

The Lord said to Moses, 'Tell the Israelites to bring me an offering. You are to receive the offering for me from everyone whose heart prompts them to give… gold, silver and bronze; blue, purple and scarlet yarn and fine linen; goat hair; ram skins dyed red and other durable leather; acacia wood; olive oil for the light; spices for the anointing oil and for the fragrant incense; and onyx stones and other gems to be mounted on the ephod and breastplate. Then let them make a sanctuary for me, and I will dwell among them. Make this tabernacle and all its furnishings exactly like the pattern I will show you.'

If you can, read to the end of chapter 27 to get the full picture as our passage only shows a part of it. It is also well worth looking at relevant diagrams and illustrations on the Internet or in Bible dictionaries to get a clearer idea of the intricacy of the instructions that the Lord gives to Moses.

After the voluntary offerings are received, the sanctuary (literally, 'holy place') is established, encompassing a range of artefacts from a tabernacle to the ark (more accurately, 'chest'), designed to hold the two stone tablets of covenant law. All the items symbolise in different ways the attributes of the Almighty for, as he promises the people (v. 8), when the sanctuary is finished, he will 'dwell among them'. The ark of the covenant, for example, was not magic in itself but sanctified as a sign of God's presence. This fact was overlooked when, centuries before Steven Spielberg brought us *Raiders of the Lost Ark*, the elders of Israel tried to use the ark as a kind of amulet to gain victory over the Philistines (1 Samuel 4), with disastrous consequences.

The magnificence of the sanctuary and its furnishings was a fitting reminder of the holiness and splendour of the Lord God. The Creator chose to be symbolised by order, symmetry and things that were both fit for purpose and beautiful. Do such characteristics spring to mind when we think of our own places of worship? Are they fit for purpose, do they welcome all ages, with an atmosphere of warmth and light (spiritual, if not material)? Are they even clean and cared-for?

Reflection

Think about what a visitor might conclude about God from a visit to your church building—then ask one!

NS

EXODUS 28:2–3; 29:38, 42–46 (TNIV, ABRIDGED)

Servants of the Lord

'Make sacred garments for your brother Aaron to give him dignity and honour. Tell all the skilled workers to whom I have given wisdom in such matters that they are to make garments for Aaron, for his consecration, so that he may serve me as priest… This is what you are to offer on the altar regularly each day: two lambs a year old… For the generations to come this burnt offering is to be made regularly at the entrance to the tent of meeting before the Lord. There I will meet you and speak to you; there also I will meet with the Israelites, and the place will be consecrated by my glory… Then I will dwell among the Israelites and be their God. They will know that I am the Lord their God, who brought them out of Egypt.'

A Low Church minister was a visiting celebrant at a High Church parish. Entering the vestry, he saw a daunting pile of vestments and hurriedly arrayed himself as best he could. 'I think that went well,' he remarked to the churchwarden afterwards. 'A lovely service, Father,' was the gentle reply. 'But in this church we do not normally wear the bookmark.'

The issue of ministerial robes can be a fraught one, to put it mildly, but in today's passage we are reminded of the underlying principle. The priest's 'sacred garments' were designed to give him 'dignity and honour' as well as (if we read on) to symbolise both his duties (rather than bestowing prestige) and the character of the God he served.

Following a lengthy consecration ceremony, the priests took up their work, which centred on morning and evening sacrifices. They were to make burnt offerings (mentioned here) and grain and drink offerings, according to divine instructions, so that God could draw close and 'dwell' with the Israelites.

The final verses remind us again that the point of the priestly ritual, the covenant and the Exodus itself is that the Lord longs for relationship with his creatures. 'God with us', 'Emmanuel' is not just an idea that crystallised at the birth of Jesus; God has always yearned to walk with us, as in Eden, and for us to know him as our Lord.

Reflection

'We have a great high priest who has gone through the heavens, Jesus the Son of God' (Hebrews 4:14, NIV).

NS

EXODUS 30:1–3, 7–8, 34–37 (TNIV, ABRIDGED)

Holy fragrance

'Make an altar of acacia wood for burning incense... Overlay the top and all the sides and the horns with pure gold, and make a gold moulding around it... Aaron must burn fragrant incense on the altar every morning when he tends the lamps. He must burn incense again when he lights the lamps at twilight so that incense will burn regularly before the Lord for the generations to come... Take fragrant spices—gum resin, onycha and galbanum—and pure frankincense, all in equal amounts, and make a fragrant blend of incense, the work of a perfumer... Do not make any incense with this formula for yourselves; consider it holy to the Lord.'

Chapter 30 also includes rules about the payment of a 'ransom' to the Lord (vv. 12–16, NIV), instructions about a bronze basin for priestly washing (vv. 17–21) and the formula for an anointing oil (vv. 22–33). This oil was to be reserved for sacred purposes, too.

The reason for the incense burning is not spelled out. Like offering sacrifices, it may have simply been part of general religious ceremonial, rather than unique to the Israelites. What was unique, however, was that this incense was burned to honour the Saviour God of the Israelites. Interestingly, when incense is mentioned in Psalm 141:2, it is linked to prayer rising to God's throne, which is echoed in John's vision in Revelation, where it is identified as 'the prayers of God's holy people' (5:8).

It is worth reflecting on how richly sensuous Israelite worship was, with smell, taste, touch, sight and sound all drawn into acknowledging 'God with us'. If our worship is too wordy and cerebral, we risk blocking off ways by which God might speak to us. Smell, for example, has been identified as the sense most closely linked to memory.

While some 'alternative worship' communities have experimented with incense, it is usually considered a no-go area for many churches. All I can say is that, after five years of attending an incense-swinging church, I found the smell certainly evoked a mood of worship—more than the smell of damp, dust and ageing hassocks, anyway.

Reflection

'May my prayer be set before you like incense; may the lifting up of my hands be like the evening sacrifice' (Psalm 141:2, NIV).

NS

Exodus 31:1–6 (TNIV)

Spirit-filled craftsmen

Then the Lord said to Moses, 'See I have chosen Bezalel son of Uri, the son of Hur, of the tribe of Judah, and I have filled him with the Spirit of God, with wisdom, with understanding, with knowledge and with all kinds of skills—to make artistic designs for work in gold, silver and bronze, to cut and set stones, to work in wood, and to engage in all kinds of crafts. Moreover, I have appointed Oholiab son of Ahisamak, of the tribe of Dan, to help him. Also I have given ability to all the skilled workers to make everything I have commanded you.'

The names of these two craftsmen have been preserved for all time, such was the importance of their role, just as the Hebrew midwives Shiphrah and Puah were remembered for their defiance of the Egyptian king's genocidal decree (Exodus 1:1–21).

What is striking about Bezalel is that he is identified as being 'filled with the Spirit of God', as if he were a prophet. The 'artistic designs' that he will create and supervise will speak powerfully of the Lord God, as do a prophet's oracles. As Hugh Page explains (*PBC Exodus*, p. 145): 'God's dwelling… is like a text, and its structures, utensils and rituals are the words that contain the key to salvation'.

God's Spirit has blessed Bezalel with gifts in working with metal, stone and wood, all highly skilled crafts; likewise the 'skilled workers' have received their talent from the same source. More than a few of them may have developed their gifts in the cultural hothouse that was ancient Egypt, but now those gifts were to be used to bring glory to the true God.

It is symptomatic of our world's lopsided values that too many tend to think of those who 'work with their hands' as somehow lower down the social ladder than the 'white collar' brigade. As churches, we need to model a different way, valuing as equal yet different those who preach sermons, provide prayer ministry and arrange the flowers.

Reflection

'There are different kinds of gifts, but the same Spirit distributes them. There are different kinds of service, but the same Lord. There are different kinds of working, but in all of them and in everyone it is the same God at work' (1 Corinthians 12:4–6).

NS

Monday 15 February

Exodus 31:12–14, 17 (TNIV)

Ordered to rest

Then the Lord said to Moses, 'Say to the Israelites, "You must observe my Sabbaths. This will be a sign between me and you for the generations to come, so that you may know that I am the Lord, who makes you holy. Observe the Sabbath, because it is holy to you. Anyone who desecrates it is to be put to death; those who do any work on that day must be cut off from their people... It will be a sign between me and the Israelites for ever, for in six days the Lord made the heavens and the earth, and on the seventh day he abstained from work and rested."'

Why is the decree about sabbath-keeping repeated yet again and, this time, sabbath-breaking declared a capital offence? Numbers 15:32–36 records the execution of a man for gathering wood on the sabbath, while John 5:16–18 tells of Jesus risking the death penalty for 'working' on the day of rest.

Today, we may well struggle with this insistence on the sabbath. Wasn't it an incredibly harsh burden to place on a nation, especially for those at subsistence level, struggling to find enough food and supplies anyway? As Tevye the milkman complains to God in *The Fiddler on the Roof*: 'I know we are the chosen ones, but once in a while can't you choose somebody else?'

What the Lord tells the people is that the sabbath is a sign (like circumcision) that they are different. Other nations may have had similar practices but, for the Israelites, it has particular significance. It is 'holy' to them, an 'eternal covenant' and links right back to creation when God himself 'rested'. The Hebrew word for 'rested' derives from the word for 'breath, life, soul' (*nephesh*). In other words, God 'took a breather', 'came up for air'.

The sabbath-keeping decree is repeated with such force because God's priorities are different. Just as they receive the final instructions for the complex tabernacle-making project, the people are ordered—on pain of death—to make sure that they rest. God did not want them to revert to the slave mentality of their years in Egypt.

Reflection

Maintaining a 'day of rest' mentality is not a slacker's charter, but recognition that we can literally work ourselves to death.

NS

EXODUS 32:1–6 (TNIV)

Travesty

When the people saw that Moses was so long in coming down from the mountain, they gathered round Aaron and said, 'Come, make us gods who will go before us. As for this fellow Moses who brought us up out of Egypt, we don't know what has happened to him.' Aaron answered them, 'Take off the gold ear-rings that your wives, your sons and your daughters are wearing, and bring them to me.'... He took what they handed him and made it into an idol cast in the shape of a calf, fashioning it with a tool. Then they said, 'These are your gods, Israel, who brought you up out of Egypt.' When Aaron saw this, he built an altar in front of the calf and announced, 'Tomorrow there will be a festival to the Lord.' So the next day the people rose early and sacrificed burnt offerings and presented fellowship offerings. Afterwards they sat down to eat and drink and got up to indulge in revelry.

Following all that we have considered in previous chapters—the holiness, the glory, the laws, the warnings, the promises—what now happens beggars belief. The people grow impatient and turn to Aaron. It's not that they are worried for Moses' safety; they speak disparagingly of him ('this fellow') and, instead of asking Aaron to pray to the Lord for their leader's return, they demand 'gods'.

Aaron, in response, gives them a god. By colluding with them, he aids them in breaking both the first and second of the Ten Commandments. Their wilful self-delusion is eye-watering as they hail the man-made artefact as the power that delivered them from slavery. Then, travesty of travesties, Aaron builds an altar for the idol and announces a 'festival to the Lord'.

When we read 'calf', we should not think of a wobbly-legged baby, but a young bull, a symbol of strength and fertility in many cultures. After offering sacrifices, the people feast (a grotesque echo of the covenant feast in God's presence of 24:11) and then enjoy 'revelry'. We might say 'got down to some adult fun', as the nuance of the Hebrew is not only 'laughter' but also 'caress', in a sexual sense. The party is well underway, but the moment of reckoning is approaching rapidly.

Reflection

We would never do anything so heedless, so sinful, so absolutely stupid—would we?

NS

EXODUS 32:19–25 (TNIV, ABRIDGED)

The wrath of Moses

When Moses approached the camp and saw the calf and the dancing, his anger burned and he threw the tablets out of his hands, breaking them to pieces at the foot of the mountain. And he took the calf they had made and burned it in the fire; then he ground it to powder, scattered it on the water and made the Israelites drink it. He said to Aaron, 'What did these people do to you, that you led them into such great sin?' 'Do not be angry, my lord,' Aaron answered. 'You know how prone these people are to evil... they gave me the gold, and I threw it into the fire, and out came this calf!' Moses saw that the people were running wild and that Aaron had let them get out of control and so become a laughing-stock to their enemies.

Before this dramatic moment, Moses was forewarned of the people's treachery (vv. 7–9). In fact, God offered to make him into a new nation (v. 10), replacing the faithless 'Israelites' with 'Mosesites', offering a fresh start and perhaps a quicker arrival at the Promised Land. Moses, however, pleads on behalf of the people (vv. 30–32) until this Plan B is abandoned. Now he has to go down the mountain and sort out the mess.

We should not think of the tablet-smashing as Moses having a temper tantrum (although his anger 'burned') but, rather, of him creating the strongest possible sign of the broken covenant. This is how the people have treated the vows of eternal fidelity that they have exchanged with the Lord God. The idol is destroyed, showing how powerless and spiritually worthless it was. As Moses reduced it to ashes, and ground the ashes into dust, there may have been some who were hoping, perhaps even expecting, a thunderclap or lightning bolt to strike him down. There was nothing, though, except a bitter drink. Worse punishment was to follow (vv. 27–35).

Rather than accepting responsibility for the catastrophe, Aaron blames others, in a way that echoes right back to the Fall. There is no trace of repentance in his reply to Moses, just the age-old whine 'It wasn't *my* fault'.

Reflection

Today is Ash Wednesday—a chance to reflect on where we have fallen short of God's standards as well as to seek forgiveness and renewed relationship.

NS

EXODUS 33:12–14, 18, 21–23 (TNIV, ABRIDGED)

Moses and the glory of the Lord

Moses said to the Lord, 'You have been telling me, "Lead these people", but you have not let me know whom you will send with me. You have said, "I know you by name and you have found favour with me." If you are pleased with me, teach me your ways so I may know you…' The Lord replied, 'My Presence will go with you, and I will give you rest.'… Moses said, 'Now show me your glory.'… Then the Lord said, 'There is a place near me where you may stand on a rock. When my glory passes by, I will put you in a cleft in the rock and cover you with my hand until I have passed by. Then I will remove my hand and you will see my back; but my face must not be seen.'

The dust has (literally) begun to settle. God has abandoned neither his people nor his promises, but things are not quite the same as before. The Israelites have proved themselves 'a stiff-necked people' (v. 3), like stubborn mules, and the possibility remains of further catastrophe. They have shown no sign of repentance, although they 'mourn' on hearing that the Lord will no longer accompany them on their journey (v. 4).

Moses is using a temporary 'tent of meeting' (vv. 7–9) before the tabernacle is ready. There he speaks to God 'face to face' (v. 11), in the sense of 'clearly and directly' (see also Numbers 12:8; Deuteronomy 5:4), asking and receiving advice for the hard task ahead. He receives the wonderful reassurance that 'my Presence will go with you, and I will give you rest'—words that have consoled countless other leaders down the years.

Then he makes an astonishing request: to see the full face of God's glory. His immense boldness is treated with compassion, not contempt. Although no one can look on the Lord's face and live, he will nonetheless reveal something of himself to Moses when he has 'passed by'. What exactly does this mean? Earthly language starts to falter when attempting to describe the spiritual, but we do know that here God promises a glimpse of his majesty to his faithful servant, as much as it is humanly possible to bear.

Reflection

How often do we pray with words akin to those of Moses: 'teach me your ways so I may know you'?

NS

Exodus 34:4–7 (TNIV)

Abounding love

Moses chiselled out two stone tablets like the first ones and went up Mount Sinai early in the morning, as the Lord had commanded him; and he carried the two stone tablets in his hands. Then the Lord came down in the cloud and stood there with him and proclaimed his name, the Lord. And he passed in front of Moses, proclaiming, 'The Lord, the Lord, the compassionate and gracious God, slow to anger, abounding in love and faithfulness, maintaining love to thousands, and forgiving wickedness, rebellion and sin. Yet he does not leave the guilty unpunished; he punishes the children and their children for the sin of the parents to the third and fourth generation.'

As part of the process of restoration, Moses has made two new stone tablets to replace the broken ones. Despite everything, the Lord is willing to give the people another chance; he will meet with Moses on the mountain once again and remake the covenant.

In reflecting on these chapters, we may find ourselves getting stuck on the punishments, the thunder, the fear, all linked to the stereotypical 'Old Testament God' who is so often contrasted with the 'gentle Jesus'. Instead, we should marvel at the infinite expanse of God's mercy. Here we read God's revelation to Moses of his very self, his name, and he is 'compassionate… gracious… slow to anger… abounding in love and faithfulness… forgiving' (v. 6). This poetic formula recurs elsewhere (see Numbers 14:18; Psalm 86:15; Joel 2:13).

As we have already seen, the Lord longs for relationship with his children, but we are reminded that his love is also strong enough to encompass punishment of the guilty. Yes, he is endlessly merciful, yet he is also unalterably just. The phrase 'third and fourth generation' is not a literal description but an idiom, implying continuation, just as '40 days and 40 nights' implies 'a very long time'. Rather than attesting to a vindictive deity, these final verses remind us of the corporate nature of sin. What we do, the choices we make, affect not just ourselves but will also leave their mark on descendants yet unborn.

Reflection

'The Lord is compassionate and gracious, slow to anger, abounding in love… he does not treat us as our sins deserve or repay us according to our iniquities' (Psalm 103:8, 10).

NS

Saturday 20 February

EXODUS 34:29–34 (TNIV, ABRIDGED)

Moses radiant

When Moses came down from Mount Sinai... he was not aware that his face was radiant because he had spoken with the Lord. When Aaron and all the Israelites saw Moses, his face was radiant, and they were afraid to come near him. But Moses called to them; so Aaron and all the leaders of the community came back to him, and he spoke to them. Afterwards all the Israelites came near him, and he gave them all the commands the Lord had given him on Mount Sinai. When Moses finished speaking to them, he put a veil over his face. But whenever he entered the Lord's presence to speak with him, he removed the veil.

The covenant has been remade (v. 10), laws given (many specifically relating to life in the promised land, such as in vv. 11–18) and now Moses has been visibly transformed by everything that has taken place. Given the harrowing ordeals he has experienced, we might imagine him to be exhausted, a shadow of the man who led the people from Egypt. Instead, he is shining!

After so long in God's presence, he is glowing with reflected splendour, a mirror of 'the true light that gives light to everyone' (John 1:9), such that others are terrified at the sight of him. To shield them from what they cannot bear to behold, he hides his face with a makeshift covering. This episode is referred to by Paul in his second letter to the Corinthians, as he contrasts the nature of the old covenant with that of the new. Moses' shining face eventually faded back to normality, but the shining glory of the work of the Spirit, bringing us righteousness, endures for ever.

Those outside the Church sometimes comment on Christians 'looking different' and, while some would dismiss this with a glib comment about 'a Christian sense of fashion', it is true that coming to faith can be accompanied by a noticeable change in somebody's facial expression. I have seen this myself on at least two occasions. Whoever draws close to the Father is changed and the longer we spend with him, the more we are changed.

Reflection

'We all, who with unveiled faces contemplate the Lord's glory, are being transformed into his image with ever-increasing glory, which comes from the Lord, who is the Spirit' (2 Corinthians 3:18).

NS

Words of blessing

'Have you counted your blessings today?' In 'A Christmas Dinner', a short story written in 1835, Charles Dickens said, 'Reflect upon your present blessings—of which every man has many—not on your past misfortunes, of which all men have some.' What, though, is a blessing? Most of us think we know, but it is very easy to take the word, and blessings themselves, for granted. 'Blessing' is much more than the collective noun for a group of unicorns!

There are two things to say about the word itself, which is two-dimensional: it has both an Old English heritage and an association with the Latin *benedicere* ('to speak well of'). Such two-dimensionality is a characteristic of modern English, since our now world-dominant language is a blend of the old Germanic languages of Northern Europe through the Saxons and French and Latin as a consequence of the Norman invasion of 1066. Thus, on the one hand, in pagan cultures, to 'bless' something was to make it holy by some ritual act, which in some cases involved marking it with blood. On the other hand, we have the idea of benediction, which literally means 'to speak well of' or to wish well. Clearly, today our use of the word 'bless', as noun or verb, involves both of these two understandings.

In contrast, Hebrew culture, from which our Bible emerges, thought of a blessing as something coming directly from God. As we shall see, God is either credited with or is invoked in the process of blessing. From antiquity, priests, as ministers of God, were able to pronounce God's gracious favour on people and on food and drink. Traditions of the Passover and Holy Communion draw on the idea that the Creator is not only the provider of the food and drink in the first place, but, as we acknowledge and thank him for it, particular meals or dishes take on a special divine significance and power. A blessing also entailed protection and conferred approval, sometimes altering the course of history.

So, as we journey into the world of blessings, from Abraham to the resurrection and beyond, let us appreciate the range of meaning there is in both society and scripture and always remember to both count and give thanks for all the blessings we receive from God in and through our common faith in Jesus Christ our Lord.

Gordon Giles

GENESIS 12:1–3 (NRSV)

Abraham's universal blessing

Now the Lord said to Abram, 'Go from your country and your kindred and your father's house to the land that I will show you. I will make of you a great nation, and I will bless you, and make your name great, so that you will be a blessing. I will bless those who bless you, and the one who curses you I will curse; and in you all the families of the earth shall be blessed.'

Do you remember the 'Tebbit test'? In 1990 the then government minister Norman Tebbit suggested that people should consider where their loyalties lay and the national cricket team they supported was an acid test of who they believed themselves to be. His comments were controversial and flawed, for, while sport does foster and heighten national loyalties, it can also be a substitute for it. Nevertheless, there is something in human nature that causes us to huddle together in families, tribes and nations. We recognise that which we share and discriminate on the basis of that which divides us from people who are really not so different from us.

For Christians there can be no basis for any kind of racial, cultural or national discrimination for, while all are sinners, we are also all created in the image of God. It is easy to say this today, of course, but, given the appalling history of racial discrimination over the centuries and Christian involvement in the slave trade and apartheid, it is never too late to recognise the universal brotherhood of humanity, as indeed did those who brought an end to such injustices. What this means is that God shows us how to read the Bible in new ways, furthering his kingdom in each and every age.

This passage looks like a personal blessing by God on Abram, and it is. It also looks like a communal blessing on Abram's family, and it is. It appears to be an international blessing on the people of the world also, past, future and present, and it is that, too. In an age of religious doubt, suspicion and conflict, we do well to remember that the three 'Abrahamic' traditions of Judaism, Christianity and Islam all look back to this world-defining moment in prehistory.

Reflection

May God give us grace to uphold the distinctiveness and truth of Christ, showing peace and respect for all.

GG

Monday 22 February

GENESIS 27:27–29 (NRSV)

The blessing Jacob stole

So [Jacob] came near and kissed [Isaac]; and [Isaac] smelled the smell of his garments, and blessed him, and said, 'Ah, the smell of my son is like the smell of a field that the Lord has blessed. May God give you of the dew of heaven, and of the fatness of the earth, and plenty of grain and wine. Let peoples serve you, and nations bow down to you. Be lord over your brothers, and may your mother's sons bow down to you. Cursed be everyone who curses you, and blessed be everyone who blesses you!'

'*Dictum meum pactum*'—'My word is my bond'—has been the motto of the London Stock Exchange since 1801. We shake hands on an offer or agreement: a deal spoken and shaken on is a deal done. Thus we connect with Jacob who, having pretended to be his brother Esau, tricked his father Isaac into blessing him. Such a blessing, which also involves the darker element of curse, could not be revoked, and sealed the future, in which Jacob became predominant.

This blessing came quite close to being a deal and expressed an intention from Isaac towards his deceitful son (perhaps no one told him about the time when Jacob conned Esau out of his birthright for a bowl of stew—see 25:29–34). It is also ironic that, later, his own sons would deceive him about the fate of his favourite son, Joseph, whom they sold into slavery (37:29–36).

The 'protective' element of the word 'blessing' remains with us, in that when people engage in life-changing decisions, they often 'seek the blessing' of close friends or family. This is not a trivial matter, for at root it is about power: blessing, permission and protection are historically entwined. To marry, for example, without the blessing of parents could entail exile, poverty or estrangement. To have such a blessing publicly legitimises the action and made it irrevocable and unchallengeable. So it is with the blessing of our Father God, who blesses us with his love and protection. His blessing is binding and irrevocable for those who seek and accept it. God's word made flesh is a blessing for us and is his bond of eternal life made manifest in Jesus Christ.

Prayer

Lord, may your blessing sustain and protect us in your service. Amen

GG

NUMBERS 6:22–27 (NRSV)

Face-to-face blessing

The Lord spoke to Moses, saying: Speak to Aaron and his sons, saying, Thus you shall bless the Israelites: You shall say to them, The Lord bless you and keep you; the Lord make his face to shine upon you, and be gracious to you; the Lord lift up his countenance upon you, and give you peace. So they shall put my name on the Israelites, and I will bless them.

Known as the 'Deuteronomic' blessing, this is probably the most famous of the Old Testament blessings. It was given by God to Moses, who was to pronounce God's peace, emphasising his personal relationship with his people. This blessing does not present Yahweh as remote, stern and judgmental, but speaks twice of face-to-face encounter. Moses saw God face to face and his face shone (Exodus 34:29). The blessing Moses received in meeting God is now extended to his people. He gives them God's blessing just as he has given them the commandments. Indeed, this blessing *is* a commandment.

God blesses them, and us, in all events. It is not up to Moses or his successors to decide when and if God's blessing on his children is necessary, appropriate or merited. The blessing is for every generation and the priests merely agents of a higher power, doing God's will, not their own. The realisation and acceptance of this dynamic has influenced ecclesiastical history and is significant for ministers today. When I was ordained priest in the Church of England, immediately someone came and knelt at my feet and sought my 'first' blessing. I barely knew what to do and it was a very strange experience. I wondered later whether my 'first blessing' should have been for a family member or friend, but soon I realised that this approach is wrong-headed. The ability to pronounce God's blessing is not a skill or perk; it is a duty and privilege to those called to do so. Such blessing is not 'done' by the minister—she or he does not bless anyone or anything, but, rather, reminds and reinforces. That person was welcome to my 'first' blessing, but it wasn't that: it was God's blessing, merely pronounced by me, then and many times since.

Prayer

Lord, shine your light upon us, for it is you alone who bless us. Amen

GG

Wednesday 24 February

Matthew 14:19–21 (NRSV)

Bring and share blessings

Then [Jesus] ordered the crowds to sit down on the grass. Taking the five loaves and the two fish, he looked up to heaven, and blessed and broke the loaves, and gave them to the disciples, and the disciples gave them to the crowds. And all ate and were filled; and they took up what was left over of the broken pieces, twelve baskets full. And those who ate were about five thousand men, besides women and children.

Have you come across 'bring and share' meals? Each person or family who comes prepares enough food for a few people, but the whole is greater than the sum and many are fed! Such communal meals embody the idea of sharing, such that you do not necessarily eat what you prepared and enjoy what others bring. Many churches do this regularly, emphasising the mutual blessings that fellowship, generosity, conversation and eating together bring. As a consequence of a willingness to share resources and trust in God, everyone is satisfied.

These meals remind us not only of the feeding of the 5000 but also the practices of the Early Church. The first Christians ate together and their meals became the first eucharists. In sharing bread and wine together, Christ shares himself with us as we join together as one large family, partaking of food, Christ and each other's gifts, talents and personalities. We behave as and become the body of Christ, and that is a real blessing to us, effected in us whenever we join together as Christian communities in meal fellowship and worship.

Holy Communion is the supper that our Lord gave us, as a permanent, repeatable and ongoing remembrance of his time on earth. Just as services today connect us with the Last Supper, the Passover feast, from which it evolved, connects it to the past as well as the future. The 'feeding' miracles (Jesus also fed the 4000—see 15:32–38) represent a link in this chain and, in this account of the 5000 fed, we see how it is Christ's blessing that accompanies the feeding. Still today, the Spirit of Christ turns a simple and, on the face of it, inadequate bit of food and drink into a blessing for his faithful people.

Prayer

Lord, you bless our food when we share; help us to share your grace. Amen

GG

MARK 14:22–24 (NRSV)

Holy Communion blessing

While they were eating, [Jesus] took a loaf of bread, and after blessing it he broke it, gave it to them, and said, 'Take; this is my body.' Then he took a cup, and after giving thanks he gave it to them, and all of them drank from it. He said to them, 'This is my blood of the covenant, which is poured out for many.'

As a priest, I am sometimes asked to bless things. There can be various motives, beliefs or spiritual needs behind the request. The desire to possess something such as a cross that the Church (acting in the wake of Christ) has blessed can be comforting and strengthening. Anyone can make or buy a cross, but (as was the case when I worked there), a cross bought at St Paul's Cathedral, blessed by a member of the clergy there and taken to another country, becomes far more than a souvenir. It can be a symbol of Christ's presence experienced in that place, an object of remembrance that betokens pilgrimage rather than tourism. That's why, in praying with the person with such an object, I pray that the person who comes to own the cross may be always reminded of Christ's sacrifice on the cross, but also that the object may be a blessing to the one who wears or bears it. Thus, it is the person, not the object that is blessed.

Blessing in the context of Christ's leading of a Passover meal reminds us that there is a sense in which the blessing of bread (and wine) is scripturally sound. It is what Jesus did and he told his disciples to 'do this in remembrance of me'. Bread and wine in the Passover were always associated with blessing: 'The cup of blessing that we bless, is it not a sharing in the blood of Christ?' (1 Corinthians 10:16). The 'cup of blessing' is the third cup of wine at a Passover meal, which relates to the lamb whose blood was shed for salvation of God's people. Jesus blesses the cup and, in doing so, indicates that it is he who is truly the Lamb of God who takes away the sins of the world.

Prayer

Lord Christ, may humble bread and wine blessed in your name become a present reminder of your saving love. Amen

GG

Friday 26 February

LUKE 24:28–31 (NRSV)

A welcome blessing

> As they came near the village to which they were going, [Jesus] walked ahead as if he were going on. But they urged him strongly, saying, 'Stay with us, because it is almost evening and the day is now nearly over.' So he went in to stay with them. When he was at the table with them, he took bread, blessed and broke it, and gave it to them. Then their eyes were opened, and they recognised him; and he vanished from their sight.

In London's National Gallery (Room 32) is a famous and oft-discussed painting by Caravaggio entitled *The Supper at Emmaus*. It depicts Christ, with downcast or closed eyes at the meal table, with outstretched hand over the food: bread, chicken, fruit. His two travelling companions and a standing figure are positioned so as to draw us into the scene. The bowl of fruit, which looks as if it might fall off the table into our lap, adds to this sense of three-dimensional inclusivity.

For our purposes, here, let us consider Christ's act of blessing portrayed in the painting. While the picture probably shows the moment when he blesses the bread (and is therefore the moment of recognition), his gesture is ambiguous. It could just as easily be a gesture of welcome as blessing, as if he is saying to us, who have recently approached the table, 'Come, do join us: sit, and eat!' His outstretched hand is not merely a gesture of blessing but also welcoming and it is this gesture by which we recognise him.

All blessings are invitations—to believe, to take part, to join in. As such, the blessing of the bread and wine of Communion is the supreme example. In blessing something inanimate, we ask God to make it something else, something more than it is. In some Anglican eucharistic prayers, we ask that 'this bread and wine may be to us the body and blood of our Lord Jesus Christ'. It is a request that we recognise and experience Jesus among us when doing 'this in remembrance of me'. It is also a recognition and an acceptance of the welcome that Christ offers when he stretches out his wounded hands to invite us to his heavenly banquet.

Prayer

Jesus, you bid us welcome to your feast. May we recognise and accept your many blessings. Amen

GG

2 CORINTHIANS 13:11–13 (NRSV)

The Grace

Finally, brothers and sisters, farewell. Put things in order, listen to my appeal, agree with one another, live in peace; and the God of love and peace will be with you. Greet one another with a holy kiss. All the saints greet you. The grace of the Lord Jesus Christ, the love of God, and the communion of the Holy Spirit be with all of you.

The frequency with which this passage is used in church contexts must rank second only to the Lord's Prayer. To many, verse 13 is simply, 'the Grace' and we say it at the end of services or to close a time of prayer or, as in the Book of Common Prayer, both. Here, in its first published use, it is a closing benediction, but it may be that Paul, in concluding his correspondence, is quoting a phrase that was already in use in the Early Church. It is, in effect, the first Trinitarian blessing we have (and the only one in the New Testament) and we give Paul the credit for it.

Paul's extended, two-way conversation with the Corinthian Christians involved perhaps five letters. It was not easy for him or them to express themselves and, while there were misunderstandings and sometimes cross words in the exchanges between them, it is good to see that Paul closes on a note of goodwill and blessing (the Greek word he uses for 'farewell' can also mean 'rejoice'). Paul's final appeal is an exemplar of Christian love, as he puts behind him past issues, even conflicts, in the genuine hope that forgiveness and fellowship will prevail.

Have you folk in your church or workplace who wind you up or with whom you disagree? Would you be able to say these words to them and mean it? If you can't, there may be a need for some form of reconciliation. In this brief passage are the foundations of not only 'the Grace' but also of 'the Peace', as used in many Communion services. The former is something we say to one another, the latter something we do to one another. The thoroughly Trinitarian benediction above reminds us that, in all things, our words should echo our actions and vice versa.

Prayer

Lord, give us grace to share and live in your peace. Amen

GG

EPHESIANS 1:3–6 (NRSV)

Two-way traffic

Blessed be the God and Father of our Lord Jesus Christ, who has blessed us in Christ with every spiritual blessing in the heavenly places, just as he chose us in Christ before the foundation of the world to be holy and blameless before him in love. He destined us for adoption as his children through Jesus Christ, according to the good pleasure of his will, to the praise of his glorious grace that he freely bestowed on us in the Beloved.

Have you ever driven down a one-way street the wrong way? I did recently and it was so embarrassing! I drove into a street, parked and then turned the car around to point the way I'd come. When I started back down the road, I was met with a barrage of flashed headlights, horns and gestures that gave me to understand I had erred, like a lost sheep, down the wrong road! All I could do was indicate apology and contrition and beg leave to go against the flow and return to the two-way traffic of the main road.

The path of blessing is easily misjudged, too. It is tempting to have a self-centred sense of what blessings are. We suppose that God bestows blessings on us, that the path of blessing is a one-way street, but, as this wonderful passage reveals, the opposite is true—the road of blessing runs in both directions. It is part of our nature and part of our Christian calling to bless God, too. We are using the word differently, of course, as we cannot do for God what he does for us, yet we can and do bless God. Blessing is a two-way street, with most of the traffic coming from God towards us, but, in a spirit of contrition, hope and delight, we offer our own blessings back. When it comes to blessing God, it really is true that it is the thought that counts! Our inadequacy is not what matters, but that we turn to God and say, 'We thank you, we praise you, we bless you!'

God has blessed us immeasurably in Christ, so the least we can do is offer blessing in return and try to walk in the right direction on the path of faith.

Reflection

God blesses us richly in Christ. It is good to know that he will accept our humble praise in return.

GG

PHILIPPIANS 4:4–7 (NRSV)

The blessing of peace

Rejoice in the Lord always; again I will say, Rejoice. Let your gentleness be known to everyone. The Lord is near. Do not worry about anything, but in everything by prayer and supplication with thanksgiving let your requests be made known to God. And the peace of God, which surpasses all understanding, will guard your hearts and your minds in Christ Jesus.

Are you a worrier? I sometimes worry that I might be… According to sociologists, we worry a great deal nowadays and young people are a particularly anxious group. They would happily tell us that there is plenty to worry about—global ecological issues, the financial woes of recent years, crime, social or racial cohesion. Serious as these issues are, I think it is true to say that some people are not happy unless they have something to worry about! At the root of most anxiety is a sense of powerlessness—the inability to control and change circumstances that pose some kind of threat to life as we know it.

The injunction in the passage from Paul to the church at Philippi represents an all-encompassing blessing. It really would be a blessing to have nothing to worry about at all, but there is a subtle difference between having nothing to worry about and being released from worrying about those things that do bother us. Paul's blessing of peace works internally, not externally. The causes of concern are not removed, but, rather, by God's grace, we can be freed from the shackles of anxiety, if and when we cast our cares on Christ in a spirit of gratitude. No problem is solved, no fear allayed, no illness cured without the grace of God, so Paul's blessing amounts to the bestowing of a gift: the gift of the ability to trust God.

All blessings, if they are to have any effect or value, involve and require what liturgists call 'fruitful reception'—that is, trust and faith in the One from whom the blessing comes. Without trust, anxieties become destructive and blessings fruitless. With God, however, there is true release, enabling us to live in hope and rejoice in his freedom.

Prayer

God, from you all blessings flow.
Give us grace to trust in your power
to free us from anxiety and fear.
Amen

GG

Tuesday 2 March

2 THESSALONIANS 2:15–17 (NRSV)

'Bless you!'

So then, brothers and sisters, stand firm and hold fast to the traditions that you were taught by us, either by word of mouth or by our letter. Now may our Lord Jesus Christ himself and God our Father, who loved us and through grace gave us eternal comfort and good hope, comfort your hearts and strengthen them in every good work and word.

Do you, or have you heard others use the word 'bless' in a new-fangled, trivial form? Perhaps you've had a conversation in which, when hearing of something cute, quaint or even moving, someone will say 'Oh, bless!' Such usage is widespread and symptomatic of two trends: the truncating of words and phrases and expressing solidarity in a way that is both sympathetic and distanced at the same time. 'Bless' simply means 'bless you/him/her/it', but to use the word as an adjective and apply it equally to poodles and poverty is surely an interesting linguistic development.

Yet, the idea that blessing involves an expression of a desire for comfort, healing or peace is neither radical nor new. We have always said 'bless you' in a semi-religious way, wishing someone well or simply as a response when they sneeze. (This latter tradition supposedly dates from the times of bubonic plague, when sneezing heralded the onset of deadly infection or represented the soul being expelled from the body: in either case God's blessing was certainly needed!) Whatever historical or modern uses 'bless you' takes on and no matter how serious-minded or trivial they are, we should, as Paul says, 'stand firm and hold fast to the traditions that you were taught' (v. 15).

It is both the Christian tradition and the biblical truth that it is Christ who heals, comforts and strengthens us. While we may appreciate the generous-spirited 'blessings' of friends and family, we should recognise them for what they are—expressions of good will for mental and physical health. On the other hand, such 'blessings' may presage the offering of prayer and that is quite another matter. Indeed, it is both beneficial and effective, for we have a God who hears and answers prayer in Jesus Christ our Lord—and that is not something to be sneezed at.

Prayer

Lord, hear our prayers for those whom we would bless and give them comfort, healing and strength. Amen

GG

Wednesday 3 March

1 PETER 1:3–7 (NRSV, ABRIDGED)

Blessed be God

Blessed be the God and Father of our Lord Jesus Christ! By his great mercy he has given us a new birth into a living hope through the resurrection of Jesus Christ from the dead, and into an inheritance that is imperishable, undefiled, and unfading, kept in heaven for you, who are being protected by the power of God through faith for a salvation ready to be revealed in the last time. In this you rejoice, even if now for a little while you have had to suffer various trials, so that the genuineness of your faith... may be found to result in praise and glory and honour when Jesus Christ is revealed.

Have you seen the light? Very soon the 100-watt light bulb will be declared extinct. In fact, you probably won't have seen one for quite a while, not at least in the shops. In 2012 it will become illegal to sell them in the European Union.

While some may feel that our present-day context of eco-awareness—not to mention financial worries—will confine us to a dimmer world, the light of Christ remains powerful. It is the metaphorical light—the light of Christ—that we need to truly shine in our lives. As Peter puts it, ours is 'an inheritance that is imperishable, undefiled, and unfading' (v. 4). This very positive nature of his praise of God is a fillip to us all. Often, we can become victims of a prevailing negativity, so it can be refreshing and inspiring to read of a hope that is not only for the here and now but for the hereafter, too!

God's light in Christ remains undimmed by the world's folly. A beacon for those who do not believe and a way marker for those who do, it continues to illuminate the path of faith. The question therefore is not how many people does it take to change a light bulb, but how much light is needed to change a person? Next time you change a light bulb, remember that, even if the world has to diminish its light for the salvation of the planet, there is an even greater power above in the God and Father of our Lord Jesus Christ and he still blesses, protects and illuminates our fragile world.

Prayer

Dispel the darkness before us on our path and bathe us with the blessed light of resurrection hope. Amen

GG

Thursday 4 March

Revelation 5:11–13 (NRSV)

Blessing and honour

Then I looked, and I heard the voice of many angels surrounding the throne and the living creatures and the elders; they numbered myriads of myriads and thousands of thousands, singing with full voice, 'Worthy is the Lamb that was slaughtered to receive power and wealth and wisdom and might and honour and glory and blessing!' Then I heard every creature in heaven and on earth and under the earth and in the sea, and all that is in them, singing, 'To the one seated on the throne and to the Lamb be blessing and honour and glory and might for ever and ever!'

We have seen how Christ, in blessing Passover wine, shows himself to be the Lamb of God, whose sacrificial act of love takes away the sin of the world. Now we read of the Lamb seated in glory, having completed his redemptive work. In the heavenly realm, it is not Christ (the Lamb) who gives blessing, but he who receives it. It indicates the natural order of heaven, where God himself is blessed by those who, on earth, he blessed in so many ways.

This vision speaks of a future glory when heaven and earth are one and 'every creature in heaven and on earth and under the earth and in the sea' (v. 13) blesses God. This not the here and now, but the there and then and we remain only half aware of the reality of that place and time. We have these visions to inspire us, but, as yet, we do not have the full picture. We do know, though, that heaven is the place of God, the hope of which is revealed in Christ.

In the heavenly realm, it is we who will be blessing God, in praise and gratitude. This suggests that, in heaven, there are ongoing experiences of delight for which God is blessed continually. Perhaps the experience of blessing God is itself a blessing to those doing it—a perpetual motion of giving and receiving! Just as we bless people for their graciousness and generosity, so beyond this life we will be blessing God for the sheer delight of his eternal presence, the promise of which he blesses us with now.

Prayer

We look forward to the day when we will bless you in heaven, O King eternal. Amen

GG

PSALM 150 (NRSV)

Everything that breathes, praise God!

Praise the Lord! Praise God in his sanctuary; praise him in his mighty firmament! Praise him for his mighty deeds; praise him according to his surpassing greatness! Praise him with trumpet sound; praise him with lute and harp! Praise him with tambourine and dance; praise him with strings and pipe! Praise him with clanging cymbals; praise him with loud clashing cymbals! Let everything that breathes praise the Lord! Praise the Lord!

Women's World Day of Prayer began at dawn in Tonga and is now crossing the world until final prayers will be said, again in the Pacific, in Samoa. In 1870, 15 years before the earliest Women's World Day of Prayer in the USA, English hymn writer John Ellerton wrote: 'As o'er each continent and island, The dawn leads on another day, The voice of prayer is never silent, nor dies the strain of praise away'. This is the spirit in which the WWDP creates a continuous chain of blessing and praise, in which everyone who has breath (not only women!) takes time to sing, read and pray together, united in a global Christian community.

There is an annual focus, a nation, whose people prepare the liturgy for the day's services, used in 170 countries. This year it is Cameroon. Perhaps you can attend a service today (or already have done), but, in any case, spare a few moments after you have read this to join the Cameroonians in prayer. They live in a land bordered by Nigeria, Chad, the Central African Republic, Equatorial Guinea, Gabon and the Republic of the Congo. Over 200 ethnic groups reside there, with the national languages being French and English. Roughly 40 per cent of the population hold indigenous beliefs, another 40 per cent are Christian and the remaining 20 per cent are Muslim. Notwithstanding this diversity, Cameroon is a relatively stable country, but still suffers a great deal of poverty.

Thus, there is much to hold before God, much to celebrate, much to ask. Remote as Cameroon may seem, today we are sisters and brothers and we have a sense, as we pray together, that, all over the world, everyone who has breath joins together in praising the Lord!

Prayer

Lord, may we breathe your spirit of unity and love in all our prayers today. Amen

GG

LUKE 24:50–53 (NRSV)

Final blessing from Christ

Then [Jesus] led them out as far as Bethany, and, lifting up his hands, he blessed them. While he was blessing them, he withdrew from them and was carried up into heaven. And they worshipped him, and returned to Jerusalem with great joy; and they were continually in the temple blessing God.

What do you say to someone as they leave your home or board a train or get into their car? 'Cheerio'? 'Take care'? 'Goodbye'? 'Bless you'? Every language has various forms of farewell, yet they all mean more or less the same thing. From 'ciao' to 'auf Wiedersehen', we send our friends and loved ones away with affection, goodwill and, to some extent, our blessing. In Spanish, 'adios' literally means, 'to God'. We offer such farewell blessings instinctively. We want to see our loved ones again and want somehow to wish them well, such that we do see them again. It is not a magic spell, but, rather, an expression of prayer for them and benevolence towards them, which we hope will sustain them and us during the period of separation. Next time you say goodbye to someone, whether it be for a day or a year, give a moment's thought to what you actually mean and what your desires and needs are.

Jesus' farewell blessing was not so different. As he ascended, he said goodbye and blessed his friends. It is perhaps strange to think of Jesus waving goodbye as he levitates heavenward and stranger still to imagine the disciples looking up and waving, but Luke's account suggests that it might actually have been a bit like that. They seem happy (unlike last time, after the crucifixion, when they hid, thinking that he had gone for good) and they go straight to the temple, rejoicing. Having exchanged farewells and blessings in the Bethany countryside, they travel the six miles back in to Jerusalem to continue their relationship with Jesus in prayer, praise and blessing—that is, in worship. For that is what worship is—the offering of worthy praise, prayer and blessing to God, who, in Christ, has blessed us with a personal relationship through which we are gifted eternal life and salvation.

Prayer

Jesus, you are your greatest gift to us, for which we thank and bless you! Amen

GG

Snapshots of Jesus in Matthew

I was clearing out some cupboards recently and found the inevitable stash of photographs. I sat on the floor, surrounded by piles of things to be sorted, looking through the pictures and reliving the events they record. The baptism of my two grandchildren, solemn and beautiful in their best dresses, with the light of their baptismal candles reflected in their wide eyes. A small snap of my long-dead father, showing off a magnificent dahlia in his suburban back garden. A professional portrait of my mother, just in her twenties and looking stunning in her white silk blouse.

When I first read the title for these readings, I began to think about the four Gospels and how the pictures of the Lord Jesus in each of them are slightly different. The focus changes, depending on who is behind the camera, as it were. Luke, the doctor, gives us pictures of healing and compassion, women and children, meals and celebrations. Mark's Gospel races along, punctuated by the word 'immediately', and is full of snaps of Jesus in action. Matthew is the man behind the camera for my project here, but what pictures has he left us?

Matthew writes for his fellow Jews. Many of them believed that the Messiah would come as the king of Israel and establish a kingdom that would never end, but Matthew realises they have forgotten many of the prophecies that also speak of rejection and suffering. He lines up his shots carefully and ensures that they are well focused. He needs to show what sort of king Jesus is, what sort of kingdom he came to establish, so he concentrates on the aspects of Jesus' life and ministry that most clearly demonstrate his kingship—his authority over evil, his rule over the natural world, the power of his death and resurrection.

Rulers, whether by birth or election, command our respect, but this is a king we are to worship and give our lifelong service to. As citizens of his kingdom, we operate under a different culture from that of the world. We are driven not by ambition but by costly service. We are rewarded not with money, fame and power but his commendation.

So, let's spend some time looking through Matthew's photograph album. Let's relive the stories he tells and see again his portrait of Jesus, the King of kings and Lord of lords, and let us work to make his kingdom come.

Jennifer Oldroyd

Sunday 7 March

MATTHEW 1:1–6 (NRSV)

The genealogy

An account of the genealogy of Jesus the Messiah, the son of David, the son of Abraham. Abraham was the father of Isaac, and Isaac the father of Jacob, and Jacob the father of Judah and his brothers, and Judah the father of Perez and Zerah by Tamar, and Perez the father of Hezron, and Hezron the father of Aram, and Aram the father of Aminadab, and Aminadab the father of Nahshon, and Nahshon the father of Salmon, and Salmon the father of Boaz by Rahab, and Boaz the father of Obed by Ruth, and Obed the father of Jesse, and Jesse the father of King David.

As already mentioned, Matthew wrote his Gospel for the Jews, for whom it was important to know who your ancestors were. To be 'a son of Abraham' was to belong, and to be descended from the family of David was to belong to the royal family.

Born in humble circumstances, living in the sticks, working for his living—none of this made any difference: Jesus was of the kingly line. As such, he fulfilled the prophecies concerning the Messiah, so Matthew begins his Gospel: 'An account of the genealogy of *Jesus the Messiah*…' (v. 1).

Whether we see Jesus preaching, teaching, healing or dying, we see a king. Not the sort of king that the oppressed people were hoping for—someone to turf out the Roman oppressors and 'restore the kingdom to Israel' (Acts 1:6)—but the ruler of a new kingdom, not of this world.

Snapshots of Jesus in Matthew show us a figure of authority. His will is law. His word is truth. His power is absolute. He is our ruler, but his rules are those of love and sacrifice and suffering. All power in heaven and on earth has been given to him, but he wields it quite differently from any earthly authority figure. As Jesus said to Pilate at his trial, 'You say that I am a king. For this I was born, and for this I came into the world, to testify to the truth. Everyone who belongs to the truth listens to my voice' (John 18:37).

Prayer

Lord Jesus, I acknowledge you today as my king. Teach me how to listen to your voice, discern the truth and obey you, my Master and Lord. Amen

JO

Monday 8 March

MATTHEW 2:1–5 (NRSV)

The nativity

In the time of King Herod, after Jesus was born in Bethlehem of Judea, wise men from the East came to Jerusalem, asking, 'Where is the child who has been born king of the Jews? For we observed his star at its rising, and have come to pay him homage.' When King Herod heard this, he was frightened, and all Jerusalem with him; and calling together all the chief priests and scribes of the people, he inquired of them where the Messiah was to be born. They told him, 'In Bethlehem of Judea; for so it has been written by the prophet.'

Matthew is the only Gospel writer to record this incident of visitors from the Eastern world coming to find a king. He does not tell us who they were or where exactly they came from, but, whoever they were, they had seen activity in the heavens that led them to go on this long journey.

Their arrival at Jerusalem and their enquiries about 'the King of the Jews' cause some consternation, for the Romans have given that title to Herod, who had been appointed the ruler of Israel. He is taken aback, to say the least, when enquiries about 'the child who has been born king of the Jews' elicit the response, 'Oh yes, we know about that. He is to be born in Bethlehem.'

Suddenly Herod sees his rule as being threatened, his title in danger of being usurped and the stability of his earthly kingdom possibly thrown into disarray. Something must be done. He misuses his authority, attempts to deceive the wise men, tries to kill Jesus and massacres the young boys of Bethlehem, as we read later in this same chapter of Matthew. The rightful king, by contrast, is peaceful, vulnerable and gentle and protected by God. By the end of Matthew 2, Herod is dead and Jesus safe in Nazareth.

No matter how the world looks today, there will come a time when 'every knee should bend... and every tongue should confess that Jesus Christ is Lord, to the glory of God the Father' (Philippians 2:10–11).

Prayer

Lord Jesus, may I never forget that, when you became a child, born in an outhouse in Bethlehem, you became my Lord and Saviour. May I live my life under your rule and authority and give you my homage every day of my life. Amen

JO

MATTHEW 3:13–17 (NRSV)

The baptism

Then Jesus came from Galilee to John at the Jordan, to be baptised by him. John would have prevented him, saying, 'I need to be baptised by you, and do you come to me?' But Jesus answered him, 'Let it be so now; for it is proper for us in this way to fulfil all righteousness.' Then he consented. And when Jesus had been baptised, just as he came up from the water, suddenly the heavens were opened to him and he saw the Spirit of God descending like a dove and alighting on him. And a voice from heaven said, 'This is my Son, the Beloved, with whom I am well pleased.'

All four Gospel writers record the baptism of Jesus by John, but it is only Matthew who has caught this tiny snapshot of John's reluctance. John has been preaching a message of repentance and preparation for the coming Messiah: 'I baptise you with water for repentance, but one who is more powerful than I is coming after me' (v. 11).

Now Jesus has arrived at the riverside and has indicated his willingness to be baptised. John has recognised his cousin's messianic status, but now he is overwhelmed by Jesus' power and authority. Jesus, meanwhile, waits patiently for John to thrust him into the water of repentance. John, however, takes a step back—he can't do it. Somehow the situation seems incongruous to him. Here is the Lamb of God, who takes away the sin of the world. How can John possibly baptise him? His knees go weak as he thinks of his own sinfulness and failings and he begs Jesus to baptise him instead. Jesus, though, knows what he is doing. King and saviour he may be, but he needs to take part in this act of obedience. 'Let it be so now' (v. 15), he says quietly, and John performs the baptism.

Why did Jesus need to be baptised? He did it to identify himself with sinful humanity (see Isaiah 53:12) and from now on—through his public ministry, his teaching, healing and dying—he identifies completely with us.

Reflection

This is not just a fairy story, like the prince who dressed as a pauper to win the bride. This is the story of a king who became *a pauper to win his bride—the Church.*

JO

Wednesday 10 March

MATTHEW 5:1–6 (NRSV)

The teaching

When Jesus saw the crowds, he went up the mountain; and after he sat down, his disciples came to him. Then he began to speak, and taught them, saying: 'Blessed are the poor in spirit, for theirs is the kingdom of heaven. Blessed are those who mourn, for they will be comforted. Blessed are the meek, for they will inherit the earth. Blessed are those who hunger and thirst for righteousness, for they will be filled.'

The next picture in Matthew's collection shows Jesus sitting, surrounded by his disciples, teaching them. Unlike the other Gospel writers, Matthew has collected the teachings of Jesus into chunks. He recognises that, as the Son of God, the Messiah, Jesus has the authority to teach, to be a lawgiver, and, at the end of chapter 7 (vv. 28–29), he records the fact that the disciples and others who heard him recognised that authority.

Jesus is teaching about the kingdom of heaven—a phrase not used in any of the other Gospels. He teaches about meekness and righteousness, about money and marriage, about eating and praying. The people who heard him were said to be astounded at his authority. Why was that?

Jesus' hearers would have been used to the teachings of their religious leaders. The Hebrew scriptures (what we know as the Old Testament) would have been quoted to them all their lives. They were surrounded by rules and regulations and the threat of God's displeasure if they transgressed any of them. Now they were listening to someone who seemed to speak from within those familiar scriptures, but who brought them alive and related them to their own lives.

It would be easy to read the Sermon on the Mount and see only 'gentle Jesus, meek and mild': the injunctions are there to be humble, forgive, turn the other cheek and give and pray secretly. We should remember, though, that these chapters contain the character and moral authority of the kingdom of heaven and those who listened to the teaching at the time recognised the right of Jesus to lay down that constitution. May we also bow to his authority and live as he commands.

Prayer

Lord Jesus, teach me with authority as you taught your disciples on the mountainside. Amen

JO

MATTHEW 8:1–3 (NRSV)

The healings

When Jesus had come down from the mountain, great crowds followed him; and there was a leper who came to him and knelt before him, saying, 'Lord, if you choose, you can make me clean.' He stretched out his hand and touched him, saying, 'I do choose. Be made clean!' Immediately his leprosy was cleansed.

There are some photographs that we keep because somehow they offer a glimpse of the real person. It may be a picture taken on a beach or at a wedding or a graduation ceremony, but it's special and we find a frame for it and put it somewhere we can see it constantly. If there is one snapshot of Jesus that Matthew might have valued like that, I think it would have been this one: Jesus reaching out in love and pity to a sick human being and saying, 'Of course I will help you.'

In chapters 8 and 9, we find that Matthew has collected together a number of Jesus' miracles—ten in total, including healings, the calming of a storm, restoring the demon possessed and the raising of the dead. His authority over sickness, the natural world, disability and death is thus demonstrated. Even as he records these amazing incidents, however, Matthew also has to record that they cut no ice with the leaders of Israel: 'By the ruler of the demons he casts out the demons', say the Pharisees (9:34).

Thus the great divide begins, between those who accept the authority of the Son of God and those who reject it. Matthew records Jesus' own summing up of the situation: 'I tell you, many will come from east and west and will eat with Abraham and Isaac and Jacob in the kingdom of heaven, while the heirs of the kingdom will be thrown into the outer darkness' (8:11–12). Although many chose not to acknowledge Jesus as their rightful king, he continued to preach the good news to them. He pitied them, for they were like sheep without a shepherd; and, in the end, he gave his life for them as well as for believers then and now.

Prayer

Almighty God, I pray for all those I may meet today who have decided there is no God and Jesus is a myth. May I know something of your compassion for them and, like you, give myself to them in service and sacrifice. Amen

JO

Matthew 13:1–3 (NRSV)

The parables

That same day Jesus went out of the house and sat beside the lake. Such great crowds gathered around him that he got into a boat and sat there, while the whole crowd stood on the beach. And he told them many things in parables, saying: 'Listen! A sower went out to sow.'

My sister and I often have lively disagreements about incidents from our childhood. We each remember different versions and, often, different incidents altogether. The cries of 'Yes, you did' and 'No, I didn't' can start to become acrimonious! If we step back, though, we can often see why each of us has a different slant on the past.

Matthew is the Gospel writer who particularly sees and understands that Jesus, the man he knew, is also the King of kings and Lord of lords, so the parables he remembers are the ones that begin, 'The kingdom of heaven is like...'. Chapter 13 contains a number of these parables and they describe the values and working of this new kingdom.

Look at this snapshot of Jesus: he is sitting in a boat that is rocking gently on the water and teaching a crowd of people. Some of the parables he explains and some he leaves for them to puzzle through. Some are word pictures from the agricultural or fishing scenes so familiar to his hearers and some refer to domestic activities, such as buying and selling, baking and sweeping. It is in the daily round of ordinary life that Jesus insists the kingdom of heaven can be found.

Our days may be filled with ordinary minutiae, but we can still live the life of the kingdom right where we are. In our priorities, our patience, commitment, loyalty and love, we show that we stand for another kingdom, another way of doing things.

Spending time with Jesus' parables is never time wasted. His word will continue to work in our hearts and minds until we think as he thinks, see things as he sees them and, above all, love as he loves.

Meditation

'Blessed are your eyes, for they see, and your ears, for they hear. Truly I tell you, many prophets and righteous people longed to see what you see, but did not see it, and to hear what you hear, but did not hear it' (Matthew 13:16).

JO

Saturday 13 March

MATTHEW 16:17–19 (NRSV, ABRIDGED)

The church

Jesus answered [Peter], 'Blessed are you, Simon son of Jonah!... I tell you, you are Peter, and on this rock I will build my church, and the gates of Hades will not prevail against it. I will give you the keys of the kingdom of heaven, and whatever you bind on earth will be bound in heaven, and whatever you loose on earth will be loosed in heaven.'

It was yet another day when Jesus and his disciples were on the road together. Once again, he had been teaching them, then he swung round and challenged them: 'Who do people say I am? Who do *you* say that I am?'

Once again, it is only Matthew who records this incident. Maybe he had been wrestling with who Jesus was, so this moment resonated with him. The words are finally spoken and the truth about Jesus acknowledged: 'You are the Messiah, the Son of the living God' (v. 16), says Peter. Jesus responds, saying that he is Peter, the rock, the foundation stone of the church, the holder of the keys of the kingdom. It seems that it is in acknowledging Jesus' identity and authority that we receive our own identity and authority and become part of the Church, part of the kingdom of heaven, part of a royal priesthood.

Whether you are in a position of leadership in the Church or not, the same is true for you. Your identity as a child of God is because of your acknowledgment of him as King of kings and Lord of lords. Your authority to act in his name is given you by him in response to your submission to him.

Peter learned this lesson, as he demonstrates in 1 Peter 5:6: 'Humble yourselves therefore under the mighty hand of God, so that he may exalt you in due time.' When a group of Jewish men, standing on a dusty road on the outskirts of Caesarea Philippi, acknowledged the authority of the figure confronting them, they changed their status for ever. That change could be seen in their lives, their witness and their writings.

Reflection

'You are a chosen race, a royal priesthood, a holy nation, God's own people, in order that you may proclaim the mighty acts of him who called you out of darkness into his marvellous light' (1 Peter 2:9).

JO

Sunday 14 March

MATTHEW 24:3–4, 30–31 (NRSV, ABRIDGED)

The second coming

When he was sitting on the Mount of Olives, the disciples came to him privately, saying, 'Tell us... what will be the sign of your coming and of the end of the age?' Jesus answered them, '... The sign of the Son of Man will appear in heaven, and then all the tribes of the earth will mourn, and they will see "the Son of Man coming on the clouds of heaven" with power and great glory. And he will send out his angels with a loud trumpet call, and they will gather his elect from the four winds, from one end of heaven to the other.'

Matthew 24 and 25 contain a good deal that is particular to this Gospel. He draws together material that is scattered through Luke, gives more detail than is given by Mark and includes three parables describing the final judgment that do not appear in any of the other Gospels.

Jesus and his disciples have been looking around the temple precincts and this has led Jesus to talk about what will happen to the temple in the future. 'Tell us more', say the disciples and so he begins, telling them of the horror, wars, oppression and suffering that must be before that lightning flash across the sky and—with a quote from the book of Daniel—the appearance of the Son of Man.

He goes on to show them how to prepare for that day by the way in which they live and he tells parables of the ten bridesmaids, the giving of the talents and the way his followers can serve him by serving needy men and women. This is not just another rabbi, teaching from the scriptures, this is the Son of Man himself. He will come back and, if we want to be prepared for that day, then we would do well to study these chapters carefully, for he will not come back as a rabbi, nor a peasant Jew. He will come back as the rightful ruler of all nations and as the judge of every human being who ever lived. Matthew can't give us a snapshot of this Jesus, for we have not seen him yet, but he has put together a collage that leaves us in no doubt of how it will be.

Prayer

Amen. Come, Lord Jesus.

JO

Monday 15 March

MATTHEW 28:16–20 (NRSV)

The commission

Now the eleven disciples went to Galilee, to the mountain to which Jesus had directed them. When they saw him, they worshipped him; but some doubted. And Jesus came and said to them, 'All authority in heaven and on earth has been given to me. Go therefore and make disciples of all nations, baptising them in the name of the Father and of the Son and of the Holy Spirit, and teaching them to obey everything that I have commanded you. And remember, I am with you always, to the end of the age.'

Each of the Gospel writers ends his story in a slightly different way. For Matthew, the words that ring in his ears are those speaking of Jesus' authority: 'All authority in heaven and on earth has been given to me' (v. 18). Today, many people find it challenging to believe that the Lord Jesus has this power and authority in the world. If it is true, why does he not do something about evil, corruption, oppression, war, famine and drought? Even in this, Matthew's last snapshot of Jesus, we can see a very mixed crowd around the risen Jesus. We can see some who worship him, but there are others who doubt, even after his resurrection. Maybe they were saying, 'So what has he actually *done*?'

For those who believe in him, Jesus has a last message—he wishes to exercise his authority, not by interfering in politics, geography or meteorology, but by sending out men and women of faith into the world. Because we believe and trust in the King of kings and Lord of lords, we can set about the business of increasing his kingdom.

So this last snapshot of Jesus shows him with his arm outstretched, saying, 'Go, therefore…' (v. 19). Whenever we dip into the Gospel according to Matthew, may we meet this figure, recognise his authority and obey his command.

Prayer

Almighty God, I praise you for the life and work of your servant Matthew. Thank you for revealing to him the kingly status of the Lord Jesus and inspiring him to record the words and teaching, life and ministry of your Son. Inspire me today with a new understanding of the authority of Jesus in my life and help me to obey his command and share what I know with others. Amen

JO

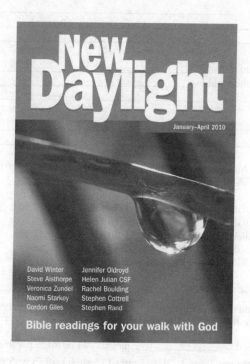

SUBSCRIPTIONS

❏ Please send me a Bible reading resources pack
❏ I would like to take out a subscription myself (complete your name and address details only once)
❏ I would like to give a gift subscription (please complete both name and address sections below)

Your name ____
Your address ____
______________________________ Postcode __________
Tel ____________ Email ____________________________

Gift subscription name ______________________________
Gift subscription address ____________________________
______________________________ Postcode __________

Gift message (20 words max.) __________________________
____

Please send *New Daylight* beginning with the May / September 2010 / January 2011 issue: (delete as applicable)

(please tick box)	UK	SURFACE	AIR MAIL
NEW DAYLIGHT	❏ £14.40	❏ £15.90	❏ £19.20
NEW DAYLIGHT 3-year sub	❏ £36.00		
NEW DAYLIGHT DELUXE	❏ £18.00	❏ £22.50	❏ £28.80
NEW DAYLIGHT daily email only	❏ £12.00		
NEW DAYLIGHT email + printed	❏ £23.40		

Confirm your email address ____________________________

Please complete the payment details below and send, with appropriate payment, to: **BRF, 15 The Chambers, Vineyard, Abingdon OX14 3FE.**

Total enclosed £ __________ (cheques should be made payable to 'BRF')

Please charge my Visa ❏ Mastercard ❏ Switch card ❏ with £ ________

Card number ❏❏❏❏❏❏❏❏❏❏❏❏❏❏❏❏

Expires ❏❏❏❏ **Security code** ❏❏❏ **Issue no (Switch only)** ❏❏❏❏

Signature (essential if paying by credit/Switch) __________________

BRF is a Registered Charity

Bible places: Babylon

A British soldier involved in recovering treasures looted from Iraqi museums said it had made him realise how important this part of the world was to the history of civilisation. Babylon—both the city and the nation—had an important role in this history, as underlined in the British Museum exhibition, Babylon: Myth and Reality. The city was south of modern Baghdad and about 150 miles north-west of Ur, which features in the story of Abraham. This nation was part of the fertile crescent of the Near East, the area called Mesopotamia, around the rivers Tigris and Euphrates. At the very beginning of civilisation in the fourth millennium BC it was known as Sumer.

Babylon as a state had varying fortunes over the centuries. Before and during the time of the biblical patriarchs, it was ruled by an independent dynasty, and was powerful and prosperous. Around 1600BC it was taken over by another group, the Kassites. By the time of the judges in Israel, another dynasty restored Babylon's prominence for a little more than a century, until the rising nation of the Assyrians took it over and made it a vassal state for several centuries. In Israel, this was the period of the two kingdoms of Israel and Judah, the period of the kings. About 700BC the city of Babylon was devastated by the Assyrian king Sennacherib, who had just spent some time besieging Jerusalem, having destroyed the kingdom of Israel 20 years earlier.

During all these centuries, Israel and Babylon probably had little to do with each other. Babylon and Jerusalem are about 540 miles apart as the crow flies, but the terrain is difficult and the only practical route between the two is nearly 800 miles long. Civil war weakened the Assyrian empire and this opened the way for a new independent Babylonian dynasty to seize back power. These were the Chaldeans and, in their time, Babylon was again rich and important. It was the time of the famous Hanging Gardens and the period in which the histories of Israel and Babylon are most closely linked.

In 538BC, the city of Babylon surrendered to Cyrus the Persian and, from then on, ceased to play an independent role in ancient politics. 'Babylon' in the Bible is used to refer to the city, the nation or symbolically—it stands for different things for different biblical writers.

Helen Julian CSF

Tuesday 16 March

GENESIS 11:1–7 (NRSV, ABRIDGED)

Confusing language

Now the whole earth had one language and the same words. And as they migrated from the east, they came upon a plain in the land of Shinar and settled there... Then they said, 'Come, let us build ourselves a city, and a tower with its top in the heavens, and let us make a name for ourselves...' And the Lord said, 'Look, they are one people, and they have all one language; and this is only the beginning of what they will do; nothing that they propose to do will now be impossible for them. Come, let us go down, and confuse their language there, so that they will not understand one another's speech.'

Here we have the first story about Babylon in the Bible—the story of the tower of Babel. Medieval artists portray it as a European-style tower (there's a wonderful painting by Breughel of a vast, rather decaying tower teeming with tiny people), but the writer of Genesis was probably thinking of a ziggurat. A ziggurat would have been a square building with several storeys, each storey smaller than the one below it, with staircases or ramps leading up to a small shrine on the top. In Mesopotamian culture, such buildings were found near temples.

Archaeologists have revealed the remains of a ziggurat in Babylon. It is 298 feet square at the base and located near the great temple of Marduk, the most important Bablyonian god. The city was his and its name derives from *Bab-ili* (the gate of the god).

A story that explained how different languages came about was a common part of cultures in many parts of the world and this is the biblical writer's version. There is a powerful contrast between human ambition—'Come, let us build ourselves a city... let us make a name for ourselves...' (v. 4)—and divine plan—'Come, let us go down, and confuse their language...' (v. 7).

The ziggurat, which had been a sign of devotion to their god for the Babylonians, becomes a sign of revolt against the biblical God. The division between people and God is echoed in the divisions between the people caused by the different languages. Perhaps we can see languages as symbolic of different worldviews, too, which make it hard for people to hear each other and work together.

Prayer

Lord of heaven and earth, keep me humble, united with you.

HJ CSF

GENESIS 11:31; 12:1–3 (NRSV)

Leaving all

Terah took his son Abram and his grandson Lot son of Haran, and his daughter-in-law Sarai, his son Abram's wife, and they went out together from Ur of the Chaldeans to go into the land of Canaan; but when they came to Haran, they settled there... Now the Lord said to Abram, 'Go from your country and your kindred and your father's house to the land that I will show you. I will make of you a great nation, and I will bless you, and make your name great, so that you will be a blessing. I will bless those who bless you, and the one who curses you I will curse; and in you all the families of the earth shall be blessed.'

Another story from the very earliest history of God's people, and one about a figure who is shared with the other two monotheistic faiths—Judaism and Islam. Abram (later Abraham) is called to leave the settled life of Babylonia, which was one of the most advanced cultures of the ancient world. There may be an implicit criticism here of this powerful and prosperous society.

Ur was a city on the bank of the Euphrates River; it's probable that Terah and his family lived not in the city but in encampments outside its walls, going in to trade and barter. They worshipped their own gods, which were not the gods of the Babylonians, but gods of their nomadic life (Joshua 24:2). So the call of the Lord was a double challenge—to change their religious allegiance as well as leave their settled life in a prosperous part of the world and set off into the desert, towards a land that they didn't know. Haran was probably known to Terah, the place of his ancestors, but Abraham is then called to leave even that place.

Today we celebrate St Patrick—one of the many saints, especially in the Celtic world, who left their own country at God's call to set off into the unknown. God makes seven promises to Abraham, and the land, descendants and blessings are the foundation of the rest of his story and important for all who call Abraham one of the fathers of their faith.

Reflection

What might you be called to leave in order to answer God's call?

HJ CSF

Thursday 18 March

Psalm 89:5–11 (NRSV, abridged)

Who is like you?

Let the heavens praise your wonders, O Lord, your faithfulness in the assembly of the holy ones. For who in the skies can be compared to the Lord? Who among the heavenly beings is like the Lord…? O Lord God of hosts, who is as mighty as you, O Lord? Your faithfulness surrounds you. You rule the raging of the sea; when its waves rise, you still them. You crushed Rahab like a carcass; you scattered your enemies with your mighty arm. The heavens are yours, the earth also is yours; the world and all that is in it—you have founded them.

Despite the rejection of the Babylonian civilisation and culture implicit in Abraham's call to leave Ur and set off for Canaan—the Promised Land—there continued to be connections between the people of Israel and the people of Babylon. The mysterious 'Rahab' is one of them.

The Babylonians had their own story of the creation, written about the time of the judges in Israel. The 'Epic of Creation' has survived and, in it, Rahab is either another name for the waters of chaos or a sea monster. She is sometimes also linked to Tiamat, who represents chaos, and is finally defeated by Marduk in Babylonian mythology. Both Rahab and Tiamat are described as having helpers in the creation epic (Job 9:13).

So, when we find in the Bible vivid passages like this one, we are seeing both the influence of one culture on another and, in this case, the psalmist making a clear distinction between the Babylonian worldview and that of God's people.

'Who among the heavenly beings is like the Lord?' he asks (Psalm 89:6). There is only one God, rather than the many gods of the Babylonians. The 'assembly of the holy ones' (v. 5), who would have been understood in Babylon as a pantheon of gods, rather like those in Greek mythology, are, for the psalmist, demoted to being members of God's royal entourage. Also, it is not Marduk (or Baal from the Canaanite pantheon) who overcomes the chaos of the raging seas, but the one who created the world and all that is in it.

Prayer

Who is like you O Lord? Surround me with your faithfulness and still the waves of chaos in my life.

HJ CSF

2 KINGS 20:12–13 (NRSV)

A good king?

At that time King Merodach-baladan son of Baladan of Babylon sent envoys with letters and a present to Hezekiah, for he had heard that Hezekiah had been sick. Hezekiah welcomed them; he showed them all his treasure house, the silver, the gold, the spices, the precious oil, his armoury, all that was found in his storehouses; there was nothing in his house or in all his realm that Hezekiah did not show them.

With this story we step into events involving known historical figures, although, as we shall see, this is theological history rather than history pure and simple.

This is the first mention of Babylon as a nation in the Bible. The background is that of the Assyrian empire as Babylon was under its rule and the kingdom of Israel had already fallen to it, after nearly 200 years of uneasy relations. Merodach-Baladan ruled twice in Babylon: from 722 to 710BC, when he was expelled by the Assyrian Sargon, and then again from 704 to 703, following Sargon's death in 705. He may well have been seeking an alliance with Judah for a revolt against Assyria and Hezekiah's illness provided a convenient pretext for a visit. Probably this visit took place during the earlier of Merodach-Baladan's reigns, but it is chronologically out of place in the biblical account of Hezekiah's reign.

The Israelite prophets normally opposed foreign alliances as God's people were to stand alone, so Hezekiah's welcome and his perhaps foolish display of the riches of his kingdom to the king of Babylon (see 2 Chronicles 32:25) are placed by the biblical writers near the end of his reign, as a sign of the judgment to come. The writer may also have wanted to make a strong contrast between Hezekiah and his great-grandson, Josiah, who restored the Law and the pure worship of God to Judah (2 Kings 22 and 23).

The reality was not so simple. Hezekiah had attempted to reform the nation's religious life and in other passages is described as a good king, but his rebellion against Assyria had brought invasion and impoverishment to his country. As is so often the case, the truth is not obvious and one-dimensional.

Reflection

How do you see God at work in national and international politics today? How easy is it to see the shades of grey?

HJ CSF

2 KINGS 24:10–12, 17 (NRSV)

Kings and more kings

At that time the servants of King Nebuchadnezzar of Babylon came up to Jerusalem, and the city was besieged. King Nebuchadnezzar of Babylon came to the city, while his servants were besieging it; King Jehoiachin of Judah gave himself up to the king of Babylon, himself, his mother, his servants, his officers, and his palace officials. The king of Babylon took him prisoner in the eighth year of his reign… The king of Babylon made Mattaniah, Jehoiachin's uncle, king in his place, and changed his name to Zedekiah.

There are some novels that I read with paper and pen in hand, to note down the complex relationships of the characters. This part of 2 Kings calls for a large sheet of paper!

About a century has passed since the last passage. Hezekiah's great-great-grandson, Jehoahaz, son of Josiah, reigned briefly, but the Egyptians captured him and made another son of Josiah, Eliakim (renamed Jehoiakim) king instead.

Meanwhile, the Assyrians had been driven out of Babylon and the Chaldean king, Nebuchadnezzar, had come to power and was seeking to extend his empire. Judah became a vassal state for three years, but Jehoiakim then revolted, probably hoping that the Babylonians, who had just failed in an attempt to invade Egypt, would not have the power to take action. Various marauding bands from surrounding countries—Chaldeans, Moabites, Ammonites—however, took advantage of the political chaos.

Jehoiakim's son, Jehoiachin, briefly succeeded him; at this point Nebuchadnezzar had had time to regroup and so arrived to besiege Jerusalem. 2 Kings 24:8—25:30 seems to be an appendix, added by an editor working during the exile. The detail that Jehoiachin was captured in the eighth year of the king of Babylon (598) points to the account being written in Babylon, where it would have been natural to date events using its dating system.

This is the beginning of the exile—the long-threatened catastrophe for the nation of Judah. The king and his household and many of the important people were carried off to Babylon, but the country retained some independence as a vassal state, with another king being appointed by the conquerors.

Prayer

Pray for those whose countries are invaded in today's world.

HJ CSF

Sunday 21 March

2 KINGS 24:20—25:2, 10–12 (NRSV, ABRIDGED)

The end?

Zedekiah rebelled against the king of Babylon. And in the ninth year of his reign, in the tenth month, on the tenth day of the month, King Nebuchadnezzar of Babylon came with all his army against Jerusalem, and laid siege to it; they built siege-works against it all round. So the city was besieged until the eleventh year of King Zedekiah… All the army of the Chaldeans who were with the captain of the guard broke down the walls around Jerusalem. Nebuzaradan the captain of the guard carried into exile the rest of the people who were left in the city… But the captain of the guard left some of the poorest people of the land to be vine-dressers and tillers of the soil.

The urge for independence is a strong one. Despite the strength of Babylon and the loss of many of Judah's political and military elite, Zedekiah started another rebellion. Once again, Nebuchadnezzar besieged Jerusalem, beginning early in 588BC. The siege was long, probably going on until the summer of 587BC. It may not have been constant as, according to Jeremiah (37:5), the Babylonian army withdrew at one point because of a threat from Egypt, but it was distressing (read Lamentations 4 for a powerful description of the plight of the besieged people). In the end, supplies of food ran out. The king and his soldiers sought to escape by night, but the Chaldean army pursued and captured them and took a terrible revenge for the revolt. The king's sons were slaughtered in front of him, then his eyes were put out and he was taken into exile in Babylon (2 Kings 25:7).

The following month, Jerusalem was punished in its turn. Its walls were broken down, all the important buildings, including the temple, were burned to the ground and the people, both those who had stayed in the city and those who had deserted to the Chaldean army, were taken into exile.

Nearly 800 years after the people had entered the land under Joshua's leadership, it all seemed to be over. Only a few of the poorest people were left, who were considered of no significance, and they were to look after the land, which had been God's gift to his people, for the benefit of their conquerors.

Reflection

Is God confined to particular places—countries, cities, temples, churches?

HJ CSF

Psalm 137:1–6 (NRSV)

Agonies of exile

By the rivers of Babylon—there we sat down and there we wept when we remembered Zion. On the willows there we hung up our harps. For there our captors asked us for songs, and our tormentors asked us for mirth, saying, 'Sing us one of the songs of Zion!' How could we sing the Lord's song in a foreign land? If I forget you, O Jerusalem, let my right hand wither! Let my tongue cling to the roof of my mouth, if I do not remember you, if I do not set Jerusalem above my highest joy.

Exile is agonising. We can see something of this in the faces of those who have been forced to flee their land and are in limbo in refugee camps. We can also see it in migrants and refugees in our own towns and cities.

This brief psalm speaks vividly of the pain of exile and, although it was probably written in the early days of the return to Jerusalem, the sense of loss is palpable. Perhaps we can glimpse how the people felt by thinking of a time that we have been in a foreign country and felt entirely alien, not understanding the language or the culture, missing familiar food and our families and friends.

God's people in Babylon were suffering all those things, but, in addition, there was the loss of the temple in Jerusalem, the loss of the place where God dwelt and where they had gone to worship. Their religious leaders tried desperately to make some sense of this dreadful experience, but could only conclude that it was God's punishment for their faithlessness. So, not only were they suffering the pains of exile but they also believed that they had brought it on themselves.

Further, the victorious Babylonians, their new masters, mocked them, saying, 'Sing about Jerusalem; indestructible, was it? And your God, whom you called almighty—where is he now?' Faith can sustain those in exile, but the faith of these people was being severely tested.

It is no wonder that, in the closing verses of the psalm (vv. 7–9), some of the most shocking in the Bible, the writer lashes out at those who have brought the people to such grief and prays that they too will suffer the same agonies.

Reflection

Are there times when you feel abandoned by God, in exile from all that has given your life meaning?

HJ CSF

JEREMIAH 29:1, 4–7, 10 (NRSV, ABRIDGED)

Hope in exile

These are the words of the letter that the prophet Jeremiah sent from Jerusalem... Thus says the Lord of hosts, the God of Israel, to all the exiles whom I have sent into exile from Jerusalem to Babylon: Build houses and live in them; plant gardens and eat what they produce. Take wives and have sons and daughters... But seek the welfare of the city where I have sent you into exile, and pray to the Lord on its behalf, for in its welfare you will find your welfare... For thus says the Lord: Only when Babylon's seventy years are completed will I visit you, and I will fulfil to you my promise and bring you back to this place.

Jeremiah is the most prominent prophet of this turbulent time of defeat and exile. This letter may have been written after the first group from Judah were taken into exile. It shows once again the complexity of the relationship God's people had with Babylon. The pain of exile was real and the desire for revenge was real, but here is a different picture.

Jeremiah saw God's hand at work in the exile and so counselled submission to God's judgment. Some prophets, though, were trying to persuade the people to revolt, even though they were living on their enemy's own land (Jeremiah 28). For Jeremiah, the exile would end in God's time, but the promise was that it *would* end. The 'seventy years' suggests several generations, but theirs was to be more than a passive waiting. Jeremiah tells the exiles to engage with the life of Babylon and, more than that, they are to pray there. This was a radical change. The God who had given them the promised land could in fact be worshipped outside that land and away from the temple, the place of his dwelling. Of course, this has roots in their own history as the patriarchs encountered God and prayed to him long before they reached Canaan and, in fact, Abraham met God in the land of the Chaldeans—the Babylonians.

The time of exile was to prove a creative one for the religious life of the people. Babylon was a place of new beginnings as well as grief.

Prayer

God of the exile, when I feel far from home and far from you, keep me praying, keep me believing.

HJ CSF

Wednesday 24 March

ISAIAH 45:1–3, 13 (NRSV, ABRIDGED)

Cyrus the surprising

Thus says the Lord to his anointed, to Cyrus, whose right hand I have grasped to subdue nations before him and strip kings of their robes, to open doors before him—and the gates shall not be closed. I will go before you and level the mountains, I will break in pieces the doors of bronze and cut through the bars of iron... so that you may know that it is I, the Lord, the God of Israel, who call you by your name... I have aroused Cyrus in righteousness, and I will make all his paths straight; he shall build my city and set my exiles free, not for price or reward, says the Lord of hosts.

If it wasn't surprising enough that the exiled people were to pray for those who had taken them into exile and for the welfare of the place of their captivity, Cyrus appears. On first reading this passage, it sounds as though Cyrus must be a member of the chosen people, anointed by God to rescue his people, but nothing could be further from the truth. Cyrus was a Persian, from the country east of Babylon. Persia was growing in strength during the time of the exile and, in 538BC, he took Babylon.

The language Isaiah uses for Cyrus is extraordinary. 'Anointed' is a distinctively Israelite title, used of the kings whom God appointed, but here it is used for one from outside the covenant community. God also addressed Cyrus as 'my shepherd', another royal title (44:28). God is also said to grasp Cyrus by the right hand, an image used earlier of Israel (41:13, 42:6), pointing to an intimate relationship with God. In another twist, however, this is also a Babylonian image. Their kings were said to have grasped the hand of Marduk, leader of the Babylonian gods, when they acceded to the throne, and an inscription of Cyrus' survives in which he says that Marduk took him by the hand and called him by name.

Isaiah, however, asserts that Cyrus has been appointed by Israel's God to carry out his plans for his people. The conqueror of the known world is, in fact, entirely at God's disposal and nothing will prevent God from fulfilling his promise to rescue his people from exile.

Reflection

Where is God surprising you today?

HJ CSF

Thursday 25 March

2 Chronicles 36:22–23 (NRSV)

Believing God's promise

In the first year of King Cyrus of Persia, in fulfilment of the word of the Lord spoken by Jeremiah, the Lord stirred up the spirit of King Cyrus of Persia so that he sent a herald throughout all his kingdom and also declared in a written edict: 'Thus says King Cyrus of Persia: The Lord, the God of heaven, has given me all the kingdoms of the earth, and he has charged me to build him a house at Jerusalem, which is in Judah. Whoever is among you of all his people, may the Lord his God be with him! Let him go up.'

These verses really belong to the beginning of the book of Ezra, where they are repeated almost exactly in 1:1–3, but they were added to the end of Chronicles, perhaps to make a positive end to the book. Although God had punished his faithless people by sending them into exile, in his faithfulness he would fulfil his promise of return.

The exile had never been total—it took place over a number of years and some people were left in Jerusalem and Judah. Neither was the return from exile total. Although the people were free to return from 538BC onwards, not all did. Because the story of Israel is so strongly linked to the land and the temple, the story that the biblical writers follow concerns those who came back to Jerusalem, who rebuilt the temple and reclaimed the faith centred on it (you can read it in Ezra and Nehemiah).

A strong Jewish community remained in Babylon, however. The people had followed Jeremiah's advice to participate in the life of the city, become prosperous and discovered that the God of Israel was still with them. It was in these communities outside Judah that much of present-day Judaism began to develop—in particular, the synagogue as a place of worship—and when the temple was finally destroyed under the Romans, it was the experience of the exiles that enabled Judaism to continue.

Today, the Church remembers another fulfilment—that of the promise of the Messiah. Mary, like the exiles, believes that what God has promised will be fulfilled (Luke 1:45) and so inaugurates a new chapter in the history of faith.

Prayer

Lord, I believe that your promises will be fulfilled.

HJ CSF

Friday 26 March

1 PETER 5:10–13 (NRSV)

A new Babylon

And after you have suffered for a little while, the God of all grace, who has called you to his eternal glory in Christ, will himself restore, support, strengthen, and establish you. To him be the power for ever and ever. Amen. Through Silvanus, whom I consider a faithful brother, I have written this short letter to encourage you and to testify that this is the true grace of God. Stand fast in it. Your sister church in Babylon, chosen together with you, sends you greetings; and so does my son Mark.

More than 500 years have passed since our last reading and we are in a different world. 'Babylon' has ceased to refer to an actual place and has become instead a symbol. There were, in fact, two places called Babylon at this time—the one by the Euphrates and another in Egypt. It is very unlikely, however, that Peter (if he is the writer of this letter, which some dispute) would have visited either. There are no records of his being associated with a church in either 'Babylon', whereas he is very much associated with the church in Rome.

It is Rome, then, that most commentators believe is meant when the word 'Babylon' is used here. It seems likely that, after the Romans destroyed the temple in AD70, many began to compare them with the Babylonians, who had destroyed the earlier temple. It was not only Christians who made this comparison—contemporary and later Judaism also used 'Babylon' as code for Rome.

Perhaps there is another reason for the comparison, too. The exile in Babylon had been a place of suffering and the Christians in Asia Minor to whom Peter wrote, as well as those in Rome, were also suffering—not from exile, but from persecution. It was not constant; nonetheless, it was very real. Peter was writing to reassure persecuted Christians that their suffering was, in some mysterious way, a gift from God. As their time in exile had brought new life to the faith of people of Judah, so God's grace would be given to support and strengthen persecuted Christians.

Prayer

God of grace, we pray for all Christians who are persecuted for their faith and for all who feel that they are in exile from you. Support and strengthen your people in their need.

HJ CSF

Revelation 14:6–8 (NRSV)

Babel redeemed

Then I saw another angel flying in mid-heaven, with an eternal gospel to proclaim to those who live on the earth—to every nation and tribe and language and people. He said in a loud voice, 'Fear God and give him glory, for the hour of his judgment has come; and worship him who made heaven and earth, the sea and the springs of water.' Then another angel, a second, followed, saying, 'Fallen, fallen is Babylon the great! She has made all nations drink of the wine of the wrath of her fornication.'

For the writer of the book of Revelation, Babylon was a very powerful symbol. It was, as in Peter's letter, used of Rome, but with more layers of meaning, all of them very negative. Not only had Rome destroyed the temple and persecuted Christians but it was also, in the writer's eyes, a place of great wealth and corruption, vice, idolatry and tyranny, backed by the military and political power of the Roman empire.

There are references that, for the contemporary reader, would have made the link unmistakable. In 17:9 Babylon was said to be built on seven hills—as was Rome. In 18:11–13, the list of imports ascribed to Babylon is, in fact, a very accurate list of first-century imports into Rome. They are in the main luxury goods and give a vivid picture of the values of the city, from glorious fabrics and jewellery to the horrors of the slave trade.

Babylon/Rome is thus the symbol of everything that is against God and God's people. Its values are not those of the kingdom as it seeks to lead people to be unfaithful to God, to commit fornication.

God, however, is greater even than this great empire, with all its power. He is the creator of the whole earth and his gospel is for 'every nation and tribe and language and people' (14:6). The confusion of the Tower of Babel was undone at Pentecost. At Babel, the people could not understand each other; at Pentecost everyone heard God's message in their own language.

The symbol has come full circle. Babylon, in all its meanings, is not outside God's plan and power.

Reflection

In what ways might Babylon be a useful symbol in your journey with God?

HJ CSF

Holy Week

These next eight days cover Jesus' journey from the adulation of Palm Sunday, on through his teaching in the temple, to Maundy Thursday and the last supper, before the agony in the garden of Gethsemane, then his betrayal, arrest and trials. We then see his crucifixion, death and burial and, finally, Easter Day. Of course, it's daunting to stand on the brink of all this, but so it should be as these are matters of life and death for us all.

For most of these days, we are using the passages set by the ecumenical Revised Common Lectionary, which is read in many churches. This year, they are from the Gospel of Luke—a Gentile writing for the fledgling Christian communities in about AD80–85.

Luke's writing has much in common with Matthew's and Mark's and, together, their works make up the three 'synoptic' Gospels. These three have similar views on Jesus' life, whereas John comes at it from a different angle. Luke still has a distinctive voice, however, standing out even from Matthew and Mark in, for instance, stressing Jesus' faith in his heavenly Father at the crucifixion rather than any sense of abandonment. Luke also seems more concerned for those on the fringes, such as the women who are present at Jesus' burial and his resurrection, than he is with the crucifixion itself.

The passages are familiar to most of us: we've heard them many, many times and heard many sermons about them. We therefore think we know exactly what is going to happen, so we need to look for ways to make them breathe again. One approach I've used to address this is to take the readings from the King James (or Authorised) Version of the Bible, first published in 1611. Many of us know this translation but might not have heard it read out in church recently. Paradoxically, the old words can draw us to the events being described in a fresh way. They can jolt us into re-examining what is happening and pondering on its significance. The language also seems more vivid. For example, 'But he perceived their craftiness' (Luke 20:23) seems more lively and profound than 'He saw through their duplicity' (NIV) or 'Jesus knew that they were trying to trick him' (GNB).

More importantly, though, whatever words we use, the truths we are looking at are unaltered: Jesus lived, died and rose again for us.

Rachel Boulding

Sunday 28 March

LUKE 19:37–40 (KJV)

Every stone shall cry

The whole multitude of the disciples began to rejoice and praise God with a loud voice for all the mighty works that they had seen; Saying, Blessed be the King that cometh in the name of the Lord: peace in heaven, and glory in the highest. And some of the Pharisees from among the multitude said unto him, Master, rebuke thy disciples. And he answered and said unto them, I tell you that, if these should hold their peace, the stones would immediately cry out.

Luke's presentation of Jesus' entry into Jerusalem—the event we celebrate today as Palm Sunday—isn't as triumphal as it is in the other Gospels. Matthew, Mark and John have a larger crowd, drawn from many in Jerusalem, who acclaim Jesus. Here, though, only the disciples rejoice. The Pharisees' response confirms this, as they refer only to 'thy disciples', as if Jesus' immediate followers are responding on behalf of all the people. It's like when people ask Christians to pray for them—'Say one for me'—and to do what they can't or won't do—go and seek God.

There is a sense here in which someone or something cannot suppress their acclamation to Jesus. If the disciples didn't, the seemingly cold stones would just have had to speak out. If people cannot fulfil their creaturely destiny and express the praise they were made to give, other parts of creation would have had to do it for them. Praising God is a gut response that we can hardly stop ourselves doing for our loving Father. To deny it makes us less than human and closes our hearts to love.

When people ask 'Say one for me', they are probably, without knowing it, acknowledging that turning to God is something we all need to do. It's not a case of dull duty, but a natural urge that we should admit the source of our life and hope. If we don't do this, if our hearts are harder than rock, the stones themselves will step in to acclaim our saviour. The poet Richard Wilbur expressed this sentiment when he wrote:

And every stone shall cry
For stony hearts of men:
God's blood upon the spearhead,
God's love refused again.

Reflection

Where can you openly acknowledge God's work this Palm Sunday?

RB

Monday 29 March

Luke 20:21–25 (KJV, abridged)

How separate is the world from God?

And they asked him, saying, Master… Is it lawful for us to give tribute unto Caesar, or no? But he perceived their craftiness, and said unto them, Why tempt ye me? Shew me a penny. Whose image and superscription hath it? They answered and said, Caesar's. And he said unto them, Render therefore unto Caesar the things which be Caesar's, and unto God the things which be God's.

Now that he is in Jerusalem, the spies sent by the chief priests and scribes try to trap Jesus with an impossible question. Of course, there is no right answer and, whatever he says, he will be open to criticism. As usual with Jesus, though, he takes on board their words and takes the conversation to a different level.

The words 'Render unto Caesar…' have inspired a huge range of responses. Some use the phrase as an excuse for being completely otherworldly, fulfilling their obligations to society in the most minimal way and ignoring the needs of fellow humans. Others go to the other extreme and see it as justification for immersing themselves in worldly business, while keeping a little corner of their souls for God, but not letting it intrude on the rest of their lives.

I don't believe that the phrase means there is to be a complete separation between God and the world, as if he isn't bothered about his creation. We know from his great love for us and his sending hi Son, that he is profoundly involve in it.

Among other lessons this ric teaching gives us, it hints at th temptation for many of us to assum that there is a 'Christian view', party line, on every detail of ou lives. Don't get me wrong, the hair of our heads are numbered an God cares passionately about us but not everything is a test of faith Alan Bennett, in his monologue *Be among the Lentils*, refers (only hal jokingly) to a vicar attending 'th usual interdenominational confer ence on the role of the Church i a hitherto uncolonised departmen of life, underfloor central heatin possibly'. There are many aspects c our lives that we simply need to ge on with, in a faithful spirit, rathe than agonising about where the stand in the whole created order.

Reflection

Love, and be silent.

Shakespeare, *King Lea*

R

Luke 21:1–4 (KJV)

Giving from our abundance

And he looked up, and saw the rich men casting their gifts into the treasury. And he saw also a certain poor widow casting in thither two mites. And he said, Of a truth I say unto you, that this poor widow hath cast in more than they all: For all these have of their abundance cast in unto the offerings of God: but she of her penury hath cast in all the living that she had.

Jesus, teaching in the temple in Jerusalem, points out to his listeners some of the other visitors. He contrasts those who donate 'of their abundance'—out of their wealth, with plenty still in their pockets—with the widow, who gives from her poverty, 'all the living that she had'. The Greek word here for 'living' (or 'livelihood', '*bios*') is the same as that for life itself, so there is a sense, too, in which she gives her life.

This tells us that giving isn't about the numerical total of what has been donated, but about the character of the giver—their approach to what they have and what they have left after giving. It's about people, not things.

At the Lambeth Conference (the gathering of Anglican bishops from all over the world that takes place every ten years) of 2008, there were people from the richest, most expensively equipped churches, worshipping and studying the Bible with those from the poorest places on earth, who had few buildings or books. How could the two extremes relate to each other?

I put this question to Jane Williams, who is married to the Archbishop of Canterbury, who was organising the programme for the bishops' wives and husbands. She said that one of the main things was just getting to know one another, getting to feel what was important to the other person and how they experienced God and the world. She knew this couldn't solve all the problems, but it was a way in. 'People begin to trust each other's good faith,' she said. 'Even if it reaches conclusions you don't agree with, you know the other people are trying to be disciples.'

Reflection

Can we put a face to our giving and give out of our abundance to those who have so little? Does your church have links with people and places in need of the basics, while we have more than we really need?

RB

Wednesday 31 March

LUKE 22:17–20 (KJV)

Becoming Jesus' body

And he took the cup, and gave thanks, and said, Take this, and divide it among yourselves: For I say unto you, I will not drink of the fruit of the vine, until the kingdom of God shall come. And he took bread, and gave thanks, and brake it, and gave unto them, saying, This is my body which is given for you: this do in remembrance of me. Likewise also the cup after supper, saying, This cup is the new testament in my blood, which is shed for you.

We are looking ahead here to the events that we will mark tomorrow (Maundy Thursday), when churches celebrate Jesus' founding of the Lord's Supper, the Holy Communion or eucharist. It's a small moment of joy amid the atmosphere of suffering and death—modified rapture, perhaps.

Among other things, Jesus here is reminding us of why this is all happening. He is doing this for us, on our behalf—but, of course, it's much more than that. He is giving us something that we can carry out to remember him and to join with him in one of the most intimate ways we can imagine. By sharing his body, we can be part of him, here and now. Millions of us across the world are brought together in this way, built up into a mighty body. We can be the hands and feet of Jesus, as Teresa of Avila (1515–1582) noted: 'Christ has no Body now but yours, no hands, no feet on earth but yours'.

The Communion service, in whatever Christian tradition we encounter it, works on so many different levels at the same time. Sometimes in church the words and actions seem impossibly rich and bewildering, while at other times they seem beautifully simple. We can become one with Jesus. We can be strengthened, fed by the nourishment of Jesus' very self, sacrificed once for us. This is something solid, which we can feel and touch. As John Chrysostom (AD347–407) said, 'Our Lord hands over to you in tangible things that which is perceived by the mind.'

Reflection

He was the Word that spake it,
He took the Bread and brake it,
And what that word did make it,
That I believe, and take it.

Queen Elizabeth I (1533–1603)

RB

LUKE 22:40–44 (KJV)

Turning from evil to good

[Jesus] said unto [the disciples], Pray that ye enter not into temptation. And he was withdrawn from them about a stone's cast, and kneeled down, and prayed, Saying, Father, if thou be willing, remove this cup from me: nevertheless not my will, but thine, be done. And there appeared an angel unto him from heaven, strengthening him. And being in an agony he prayed more earnestly: and his sweat was as it were great drops of blood falling down to the ground.

Gethsemane speaks to each of us directly about those moments when we think something like, 'If only I didn't have to go through this. Please, God, take it away.' Maybe it is an operation, childbirth, an interview, a difficult meeting or some other seemingly impossible trial. Even if there is no way out of enduring the terror, as there was no escape for Jesus, there are crumbs of comfort in both God's presence with us and the knowledge that Jesus has been here, too, and can empathise with us: 'one who in every respect has been tested as we are' (Hebrews 4:15, NRSV).

Sometimes, though, this just doesn't seem enough and we really can't cope. It is then that we have to throw ourselves on God, pray hard and look for the support of other people. Often, it is not the one-off crisis or decision that brings us to breaking-point, but the relentless dull ache of having to keep going—perhaps because of illness, lack of money, difficult relationships or intractable people. At such times we have to try, if only feebly, one step at a time, to turn to the good wherever we can.

It reminds me of a part in *Persuasion* by Jane Austen where the heroine visits an old schoolfriend who, despite serious illness limiting what she can do, still manages to be positive and even generous to others:

A submissive spirit might be patient, a strong understanding would supply resolution, but here was something more; here was that elasticity of mind, that disposition to be comforted, that power of turning readily from evil to good, and of finding employment which carried her out of herself... It was the choicest gift of Heaven.

Prayer

Heavenly Father, help me to turn to you in times of trouble. Carry me through the pain.

RB

Friday 2 April

Luke 23:44–47 (KJV)

Reaching out to us in love

And it was about the sixth hour, and there was a darkness over all the earth until the ninth hour. And the sun was darkened, and the veil of the temple was rent in the midst. And when Jesus had cried with a loud voice, he said, Father, into thy hands I commend my spirit: and having said thus, he gave up the ghost. Now when the centurion saw what was done, he glorified God, saying, Certainly this was a righteous man.

Luke's treatment of the crucifixion is not as bleak as Mark's or Matthew's (the two other Gospels that are closest to his). Jesus does not cry out in desolation that his Father has forsaken him. Instead, he prays for his tormentors—'Father, forgive them…' (v. 34) and reassures the penitent thief: 'Today shalt thou be with me in Paradise' (v. 43).

Luke focuses on Jesus' resignation, which here is almost serenity, as he gives himself to his Father, using the words of Psalm 31:5 ('into thine hand…'). He accepts his torture quietly. This is a confident surrender, firm in the hope accompanying it. The world might not understand, but his action is the opposite of cowardice or being a doormat. It is realistic facing up to suffering and a refusal to retaliate (even if he was outnumbered and couldn't have fought back, he could have exchanged violent words, but he chose not to).

This is very much the same Jesus whom Luke has presented throughout his Gospel. His true natur shines through. He is welcoming t the penitent thief, as he had bee welcoming to other outsiders, suc as women, tax-collectors and vari ous sinners. This means that ther is less emphasis on the cross a an isolated phenomenon and mor on it as being a continuation an culmination of Jesus' life. It's hi whole life as well as his death tha are our pattern and inspiration.

Jesus has done nothing but goo and here he is paying the ultimat price as if he were evil. He stretche out to us in love and we—or ou representatives, at any rate—kic him in the face.

Reflection

His gracious hands,
ne'er stretched but to do good,
Are nailed to the infamous wood:
And sinful Man does fondly bind
The arms, which he extends
t'embrace all human kind.

Abraham Cowley, *Christ's Passior*

RL

Luke 23:48–56 (KJV, abridged)

Waiting between death and hope

And all the people that came together to that sight, beholding the things which were done, smote their breasts, and returned. And all his acquaintance, and the women that followed him from Galilee, stood afar off, beholding these things. And, behold, there was a man named Joseph, a counsellor; and he was a good man... This man went unto Pilate, and begged the body of Jesus. And he took it down, and wrapped it in linen, and laid it in a sepulchre... And the women... returned, and prepared spices and ointments; and rested the sabbath day according to the commandment.

This feels like the tidying up of loose ends. As with so many tasks after a death, there is an overwhelming feeling of going through the practicalities, perhaps being grateful to have something to do in order to avoid the well of emptiness Jesus' death created.

The disciples were in that bleak state of waiting around, but not expecting anything to happen. The fact that we know what is going to happen next shouldn't stop us from pausing here and waiting with them. We have from the end of church on Good Friday, depending on when we next go to church, until either the Easter Vigil service tonight or when we wake up on Easter morning.

This is a special time, which can give us a sense of being between two worlds. There is the world of sin, suffering and death, where retaliation, casual violence and thoughtless cruelty are routine. There is also before us, in the distance, the world of almost unimaginable hope. Here now, though, there is only the waiting. It is like a miniature version of our life, waiting for the second coming. As W.H. Auden (1907–1973) says in his play *For the Time Being*, we live 'between the times' of Jesus' coming to earth and his coming again.

In this state, we can only turn to God, in the sure and certain hope of the resurrection. It might seem incredible now, in the middle of grief, but it will come.

Reflection

Be near me when my light is low,
When the blood creeps,
and the nerves prick
And tingle; and the heart is sick,
And all the wheels of Being slow.

Alfred, Lord Tennyson, *In Memoriam* (1849), written after his best friend died

RB

LUKE 24:1–6 (KJV, ABRIDGED)

Miracles can happen

Now upon the first day of the week, very early in the morning, they came unto the sepulchre, bringing the spices which they had prepared... And they found the stone rolled away from the sepulchre. And they entered in, and found not the body of the Lord Jesus. And it came to pass, as they were much perplexed thereabout, behold, two men stood by them in shining garments: And as they were afraid, and bowed down their faces to the earth, they said unto them, Why seek ye the living among the dead? He is not here, but is risen.

In Luke, the resurrection seems particularly mysterious. The women visit the tomb to anoint Jesus' body and it is clear from these and later verses that they have precious little clue as to what is happening. It will take a great miracle to turn them away from the ever-deepening furrows of their grief at Jesus' death and towards the amazing, undreamt-of future, for which they have no pattern and no expectation, but miracles do happen.

The resurrection happened. Jesus rose from the dead and is risen. Other kinds of resurrections can happen today, too, in the world and in our own lives. Many doubted that apartheid would end in South Africa or that the Iron Curtain would fall or that a mixed-race man could become president of the United States, but these things happened. Some of us don't really believe that positive change can come about for us personally. Perhaps we don't think that we'll ever be able to cope with illness or hardship or without one special person. There seems to be no hope and we would rather stay among the dead than seek the living or the living God, but God can draw goodness out of the bleakest situation. He has done it before and will do so again.

Archbishop William Temple (1881–1944) summed up the importance of resurrection, as distinct from immortality:

The method of all non-Christian systems is to see an escape from the evils and misery of life. Christianity seeks no escape, but accepts these at their worst, and makes them the material of its triumphant joy. That is the special significance in this connection of the Cross and Resurrection of Jesus Christ.

Praise

Alleluia, he is risen!

RB

Despair to joy: the significance of the resurrection

The resurrection of Jesus is the event upon which all other events of the Gospel stories are built, the indispensable foundation stone of the Christian faith and the first sign of the new creation that awaits us beyond this life. The trouble is that, like so many stories in the Gospels, we know it rather too well. That is, we think we know what it means and we've therefore stopped looking at it properly.

In this set of readings I have tried to hold back from moving through the story too quickly. Over the course of the next two weeks, we will follow the story of the first Easter as it is told in John's Gospel. On some days we will only look at a single verse, but each day we will be invited to make a leap of the imagination that will help us hear the story as if for the first time. We will go with Mary to the tomb. We will experience her shock and her emptiness at the death of Jesus and the desolation of his grave. We will stare inside that empty tomb and try to make sense of what has happened. We will wait outside and weep. We will hear Jesus speak to us. We will piece the story together.

By doing this, we will discover the astonishing outcome of that story and experience something of what Mary Magdalene and those first disciples experienced—for they were not expecting a resurrection. In fact, we miss the point entirely if we imagine that they were just hanging around waiting for Jesus to be raised. Neither was it the case that people in the ancient world believed in resurrection and so found the story of Jesus' resurrection easy to believe. Even those Jews who did hope for a resurrection saw it as being way off in the future, not something that could be experienced in their own lifetimes. In other words, the resurrection was as shocking and unexpected for people then as it is for us now, but to get that sense of shock and surprise we must enter into the story deeply and gradually. The Bible lets us do this, provided we don't rush.

For the first followers of Jesus, everything had ended in utter defeat. They were broken, disillusioned. The joy of the resurrection arises precisely from the despair of the grave. Only by waiting at the grave and seeing its desolation will we experience the joy and discover the surprise.

Stephen Cottrell

Monday 5 April

John 20:1 (NRSV)

The dark shadows of death

Early on the first day of the week, while it was still dark, Mary Magdalene came to the tomb and saw that the stone had been removed from the tomb.

Because we know the end of the story so well, we rarely linger on the most important details or the impact of the way each Gospel writer tells the story. For John, it all happens in darkness: as Judas departs from the table, we are told it is dark (13:30), when Jesus is arrested, it is night and when he is crucified, darkness covers the earth. Now, Mary Magdalene comes to the tomb very early on the first day of the week, while it is still dark.

The other Gospels mention other women, but John makes this first appearance of the risen Christ a one-on-one encounter between Mary and Jesus. Let us not rush ahead of ourselves, however. Even though we have just celebrated the joy of the resurrection, let us get back inside the fear and dismay that must have overwhelmed the first followers of Jesus as they watched his mission unravel. They saw him forcefully arrested, stripped and beaten, convicted on some trumped-up charges and—most troubling of all—silent before his accusers. It must have seemed to them that he had the best chance ever, in front of both Pilate and to Caiaphas, to demonstrate and explain who he was and what he was about, but there was nothing—just silence and darkness. Then there was his death, gruesome and painful and, at that time, seemingly bereft of meaning. All they could do was cherish their memories of him and carry out the important duties that accompanied every death: paying last respects, preparing the body with myrrh and spices.

Pause. In your imagination, hear Mary's footsteps as she makes her way to the tomb in the darkness of the first Easter morning. Imagine her thoughts and fears. See how they connect with our own inner darkness and the gnawing sadness that sometimes grips our heart when faith feels so fragile that it may disintegrate altogether, as if Jesus is, after all, forever dead. Then picture the horror of another cruel twist: arriving at the tomb to find that the stone keeping Jesus' body safe inside the tomb has been rolled away.

Prayer

Loving God, into our darkest shadows speak your words of hope and let your light break in.

SC

JOHN 20:2 (NRSV)

Desolation

So she ran and went to Simon Peter and the other disciple, the one whom Jesus loved, and said to them, 'They have taken the Lord out of the tomb, and we do not know where they have laid him.'

Mary's first thought (indeed, everyone's first reaction to these inexplicable events) is obvious and very human: the body must have been taken. In Matthew's account, a guard is placed at the tomb so that no one can steal the body and then claim that something miraculous has happened (27:64). John, however, does not speak of a guard, only the stone having been moved and the emptiness.

The point here is that no one was expecting a resurrection. As mentioned in the introduction, we sometimes imagine that people back then all believed in resurrection after death and were half expecting something like this to happen. Despite Jesus' own words about the resurrection, this was not something that his first disciples either understood or expected because the prevailing view in the ancient world was pretty similar to ours today: death is death; it is the end.

Some believed in a sort of disembodied soul that existed beyond death. Some Jews believed in a general resurrection at the end of time, but the Sadducees didn't believe even this, denying any kind of future life beyond the earthly one. Therefore, for Jesus' followers, his crucifixion put an end to their hopes. They believed that Jesus was a Messiah for this life and for this world only. His being killed, they thought, proved that they'd got it wrong—a real Messiah wouldn't have got himself crucified! Jesus, though, was not the Messiah they were expecting and the biggest surprise was yet to come.

On that dark morning, all Mary could do was stare into the emptiness with anger and regret and think that it had all gone wrong. Even his body had been taken away. In her despair she did what we human beings always do in times of trouble: she turned to others for help. She went to find Peter and the other disciple and asked them if they knew what had happened.

Prayer

Creator God, when hope is taken from us, when we look at what was and can't see what will be, change our minds and help us see the presence in the absence.

SC

JOHN 20:3–5 (NRSV)

Questions

Then Peter and the other disciple set out and went towards the tomb. The two were running together, but the other disciple outran Peter and reached the tomb first. He bent down to look in and saw the linen wrappings lying there, but he did not go in.

More footsteps, but these are more urgent. Peter and the other disciple run to the tomb. Having received Mary's dreadful message that the tomb is empty and the body has probably been taken, they have rushed there to see for themselves. Is there some hope flickering inside them at this point? We cannot tell.

One disciple outruns the other and gets there first. He looks in but does not go inside. Isn't this often the case? We are drawn towards the scene, but we hold back. Fear and dismay paralyse us. Many people are drawn to the Christian message and attracted by the person of Jesus, yet they circle around the story, looking at it from the outside. In order to understand it, though, you have to go in.

That is exactly what the two disciples are about to do. They are about to stumble on the greatest truth of human history. Right now, though, their minds are still in darkness. So, let us not rush the story; let us weigh and savour each detail and imagine that it is we who are standing outside the tomb.

We are confused. It is dark, but around us dawn is building in the sky and the first fingers of light are beginning to break up the darkness.

We are outside the tomb. We can see that the stone has been rolled away. The tomb is empty. Something has happened, but we don't know what it is. The obvious human explanation is that someone has stolen the corpse. But there is something else gnawing away at us, whispering inside. Just as shafts of light are beginning to fill the sky and illuminate the world, so something is dawning within, suggesting something else, creating a different picture.

Prayer

Steadfast God, when we are fearful of taking the next step and where it will take us, give us the courage we need to move forward. Help us to listen to your voice within us. Help us to see the light dawning in the darkness.

SC

JOHN 20:6–10 (NRSV)

The beginning of an answer

Then Simon Peter came, following him, and went into the tomb. He saw the linen wrappings lying there, and the cloth that had been on Jesus' head, not lying with the linen wrappings but rolled up in a place by itself. Then the other disciple, who reached the tomb first, also went in, and he saw and believed; for as yet they did not understand the scripture, that he must rise from the dead. Then the disciples returned to their homes.

Typically, it is Simon Peter who goes in first—and, just as typically, he doesn't get it. Throughout the Gospel story we see Peter promising much but delivering little. Is this because he wants to *do* something rather than *receive* something? He stands in the empty tomb, but there is nothing he can do. He sees the linen wrappings. He sees the absence of Jesus' body, but there is not yet any presence for him.

Then the other disciple goes in—the one whom John mysteriously names 'the beloved' but whom we understand to be John himself. He had reached the tomb before Peter, but whereas Peter is confident, John is cautious. He waits for a moment, but, when he followed Peter inside, we are told, 'he saw and believed' (v. 8).

This is an astonishing moment. John believes, but we don't know what he believes. None of them yet understands 'that [Jesus] must rise from the dead' (v. 9) and that this rising is a proper understanding of scripture. John is preparing us for the most climactic event of all: the resurrection. Our understanding of what has happened to Jesus, and who he is, is about to be reconfigured. What seemed like a failure is about to be turned into a triumph. God has raised Jesus to new life: his death and resurrection were what God had always intended. That is why John tells the story with reference to its fulfilling scripture (what we call the Old Testament; see, for instance, John 19:28, 37).

The final revelation is not given to John or to Peter, however. There is another twist. The revelation is given to Mary—a woman and an outsider. The two disciples tramp home, musing on all that has happened, still not understanding. Mary waits, and her patient waiting is soon rewarded.

Prayer

Faithful God, we have not seen. Help us still to believe.

SC

JOHN 20:11–13 (NRSV)

Why are you weeping?

But Mary stood weeping outside the tomb. As she wept, she bent over to look into the tomb; and she saw two angels in white, sitting where the body of Jesus had been lying, one at the head and the other at the feet. They said to her, 'Woman, why are you weeping?' She said to them, 'They have taken away my Lord, and I do not know where they have laid him.'

Mary stays. She wept at the foot of the cross and here, too, she stands weeping outside the tomb. All she has is her grief. All that she hoped Jesus would be has been confounded. Like the others, she had really begun to think he might be the Messiah, the one long-promised by God, but she has been proved wrong. His death just shows how foolish and mistaken she had been. This hasn't stopped her loving him, though. It hasn't taken away the good he did and the beauty of what he said, but he was not what she had hoped. He was not the Messiah.

Here, she simply wanted to pay her last respects and attend to his body and even that was denied her. So, the tears that had been locked inside her for three days come bursting out, a flood of anguish. Then, as she looks into the tomb, to her amazement she sees two angels sitting where Jesus' body had been. 'Why are you weeping?' they ask (v. 13). The grief overwhelms her and she cries out angrily. After all, isn't that the stupidest question in the world? 'Why are you weeping?' Well, isn't it obvious? 'They have taken away my Lord, and I do not know where they have laid him,' she tells them (v. 13).

Mary's anguished words reflect our own experience. When things go wrong in life, when hopes are dashed, when darkness circles, we cry out. We don't know where God is; he seems so absent; we don't know where to find him and we even wonder if there is any hope to be found at all. Meaning has drained from life; we are stranded in painful isolation, staring into the abyss of an empty tomb.

Prayer

Patient God, even when we have nothing left to do but wait, in pain, give us hope as we wait and the final promise that remaining is rewarded.

SC

JOHN 20:14 (NRSV)

First sight

When she had said this, she turned round and saw Jesus standing there, but she did not know that it was Jesus.

Mary turns and sees, but doesn't see, just like all those others in the Gospels who have ears to hear, but don't hear and eyes to see, but don't see.

Jesus is standing before her, but Mary doesn't know that it is him. Perhaps the early morning sun is in her eyes? Perhaps her tears have blurred her vision? Or is it something else? There is continuity and discontinuity. The one who stands before her is the same Jesus who was nailed to the cross, but at the same time he is not the same. She is not seeing a corpse brought back to life, someone like Lazarus, destined to die again. Although she doesn't know it, Mary is looking at the first piece in the jigsaw of the new creation; the first piece of an incorruptible physicality. It is as if a piece of the future—that promise which is the inheritance of all who follow Christ—is brought into the present to show us the way.

That is the outward reality: not an absurd contradiction of the rules of nature, but the sign and starting point of a new creation. The stone that was rejected is the cornerstone of a new building (see Psalm 118:22).

There is another reality, too. It is an inward reality about the choices each of us must make. People don't recognise Jesus today. If it was obvious who he is and what he has done, our response would also be obvious and perfunctory, but what God has done for us in Christ is done for love. What God longs for in return is love and, for love to be real, it has to be free. Take away a tiny bit of that freedom and you annihilate the love. Therefore, God takes the risk—even at the resurrection—of not being recognised. What he longs for is for us to respond freely with love, so he will wait at our side, unrecognised. He calls out to us, but he will not force us into giving a response. Love 'does not insist on its own way' (1 Corinthians 13:5); love waits.

Prayer

O Jesus, wait for us to recognise you.

SC

Sunday 11 April

JOHN 20:15 (NRSV)

Whom are you seeking?

Jesus said to her, 'Woman, why are you weeping? For whom are you looking?' Supposing him to be the gardener, she said to him, 'Sir, if you have carried him away, tell me where you have laid him, and I will take him away.'

The risen Jesus speaks for the first time and he asks two astonishing questions. First, he repeats the question asked by the angels, thus speaking directly into Mary's despair. What had seemed such a stupid question moments before is now the most beautiful. It indicates the depths of grief that Jesus has plumbed. He sees and feels the sorrow that anchors Mary to the empty tomb. She is rooted to the spot, unable to turn her face from the loss or her heart from the pain. A world that was so full of promise for her a few short days ago is now a place of desolation. In seeing and feeling Mary's sorrow, Jesus sees and feels the sorrow of the world. This is a place where all of us must stand, weeping helplessly at the graves of our loved ones, wondering if there is any meaning to life, any hope in death.

Then comes the question on which every other question hangs: 'For whom are you looking?' It reaches within the despair to its potential cure. Not just 'What are you hoping for?' but 'Whom?' Is there one in whom our restless yearnings can find rest? One who is secure, reliable, trustworthy; one who can love without equivocation or guile? Is there a person who can show me how to live without regret? Dare I hope for one who is merciful and just; who forgives and forgives again?

Something in his voice awakens Mary to her lost hope, so she cries out with her question: 'Sir, if you have carried him away, tell me where you have laid him, and I will take him away.' Her hope is for Jesus: he is the one she is looking for. He is the one all human hearts long for, though he is still unrecognised by so many. He stands before them calling their name, but they don't hear him. They think he's someone else.

Prayer

Searching God, you know who I am looking for and, even though I have often looked in the wrong places and the wrong faces, find me.

SC

JOHN 20:16 (NRSV)

The moment of recognition

Jesus said to her, 'Mary!' She turned and said to him in Hebrew, 'Rabbouni!' (which means Teacher).

Mary has railed against the man in the garden, as if she were beating her fists against death itself. She wonders if he can tell her where the body of Jesus has been taken. Yes, of course it is Jesus she is looking for. Her hopes have not been entirely extinguished by her grief, but there is nothing she can do about it, except to cry and finish the one job she came to do—anointing and dressing his body properly for burial.

Then everything changes. A whole new world is born, brought to life by the uttering of a name and a response of recognition in a world bruised and broken by anonymity, random violence and hurtfulness. Jesus speaks her name and joy—the joy of knowing and being known, of recognising and being recognised—is planted in the desert of her despair.

This man is a gardener, but not the hired hand sweeping up the leaves in the municipal cemetery. He is the new Adam, the one who will bring order and fruitfulness to God's creation. She tastes the joy of the resurrection, the future hope of humanity.

Jesus speaks her name—Mary—and her eyes are opened, her ears unblocked. As she hears her name spoken, she at last turns away from the hopeless emptiness of the tomb and towards the one who is her hope, the risen Saviour, a piece of God's future rooted in the here and now. 'Rabbouni!' she says, which means 'Teacher'. It is a friendly word of recognition. It is the name she would have used when she was with him on the road.

Now we must be silent again. The Lord addresses us with the same questions and with the same affirmation of love. Why are we weeping? What are the great sadnesses of our lives? Who are we looking for? Where do we place our hope and in whom? Then, right into the centre of where each of us is hurting the most and where we each feel most isolated, most alienated, he calls us by name.

Prayer

Tender God, you know us by name. Help us to reach out to you and to each other with the same love that you have shown us through Christ.

SC

Tuesday 13 April

JOHN 20:17 (NRSV)

My God and your God

Jesus said to her, 'Do not hold on to me, because I have not yet ascended to the Father. But go to my brothers and say to them, "I am ascending to my Father and your Father, to my God and your God."'

When Mary says 'Rabbouni!', it speaks of continuity: this Jesus standing before her is the same person she saw crucified. As we have noted, however, the resurrection of Jesus is not like the raising of Lazarus. Jesus is alive with a different sort of life, continuous with what has gone before, but also radically different. Lazarus rose from his tomb, still stinking of death's decay and struggling with the grave cloths that bound him. Jesus rose with the dawn of a fresh, clear day, the grave cloths that bound him neatly folded. Lazarus rose to die again; Jesus rose to a new, eternal life.

With joy, Mary holds on to Jesus. What could be more natural? The one who was lost has been found. She wraps him in her arms. She isn't going to let him go again.

There is more to learn, though, because here there is also discontinuity. Mary clings to the Jesus she knew in his earthly ministry, but she is also holding what we can only describe as the first piece of the new creation, formed out of the death of the old. He is the same Jesus, but the seed that lay dead and buried in the ground has now risen, with a new life that cannot be clung to in the same way. This does not mean that the risen Jesus is a ghost: what Mary holds was still matter. Later, Thomas will be invited to touch and hold this same risen body that Mary is told to relinquish.

Jesus' risen body is a sign of two things. First, the newness of the life that is continuous with the old, but is now incorruptible. Second, it signifies an inner meaning: 'do not think that you can define or constrain me'. This new life also means a new presence. Jesus points beyond the event of his rising to an unconstrained availability, which is the presence of his Spirit.

Prayer

Omnipotent God, save me from trying to contain you. Hold me and expand me and, when I am feeling small, protect me.

SC

JOHN 20:18 (NRSV)

I have seen the Lord

Mary Magdalene went and announced to the disciples, 'I have seen the Lord'; and she told them that he had said these things to her.

God's future breaks into the present. For the next 40 days, the risen Jesus will be seen and experienced by many people, within their everyday world of time and space—just as Mary has seen and experienced Jesus at the tomb. But these appearances will come to an end. Then there will be the new experience of Jesus as the Spirit, and the birth of a Church charged with a gospel of joy to share with a broken world. Mary Magdalene is the first witness—the first person to tell this good news, the apostle to the apostles.

If anyone still questions the truth of this story, ask this: would anyone making up such a story choose a woman like this to be its central witness? No, it is Jesus who commissions her. He points her back into this life and to the proclamation that will form the mission of his Church. She must tell the brothers that Jesus is ascending to the Father, but note this: the Father of Jesus is now *their* father as well.

Of course, there is still a temptation to cling to Jesus. How many of us hold on to experiences of God from the past, but have stopped looking for where he might be today?

So, where *is* Jesus today, in this Easter season for those of us reading these notes? Well, he has ascended to the Father, who is now our Father, too. At the same time, he is waiting for us in the world. We are the ones charged with his message of hope and new life. When our lives reflect his life, his risen life will be manifest in us. Then others will have their eyes opened and their ears unstopped. By recognising him in us, they will come to recognise the God who is their God and the Father who is their Father.

This is the mission of the Church: to bear witness to the resurrection of Christ. What is our proclamation? Simply this, in the words of Mary Magdalene: 'I have seen the Lord' (v. 18).

Prayer

O God of community and pilgrimage; put your words on my lips and your love in my heart.

SC

JOHN 20:19–20 (NRSV)

Peace be with you

When it was evening on that day, the first day of the week, and the doors of the house where the disciples had met were locked for fear of the Jews, Jesus came and stood among them and said, 'Peace be with you.' After he said this, he showed them his hands and his side. Then the disciples rejoiced when they saw the Lord.

The action shifts to the evening and back to the disciples. Mary has told them what she has seen but we don't know how they have responded. What we do know is that they have locked themselves away. They still seem enveloped by grief: the wrong decisions, the prevarication and the lies that led them to abandon Jesus when he hung on the cross still weigh them down. Fear—that what happened to Jesus might happen to them—has prevented them from receiving Mary's message properly. To emphasise the point, John tells us that it is evening.

Jesus then appears for the second time. He enters the room and stands among them, despite the locked doors, as a light in the darkness. Again, we are not told their reaction, although we can imagine their fear and surprise. They thought it was all over, but it is only just beginning!

Jesus greets them: 'Peace be with you,' he says. It was a common greeting, the sort of thing people would say to each other each day as they met. It also sums up the whole purpose of God's mission. Jesus came to bring God's peace to the world, to restore what was lost, to bring unity and harmony to the creation. 'He is our peace,' says the letter to the Ephesians (2:14). 'The peace I give is a gift the world cannot give,' said Jesus himself on the night before he died (John 14:27, NLT).

In telling the story, John again emphasises the continuity with what has gone before. Jesus shows them his wounds, proving that he is the same person who was killed on the cross, but alive with a new life. Only now, in the whole story of Easter, the word 'joy' is used for the first time. The disciples rejoice as they see and recognise the Lord.

Prayer

O generous God, thank you for the blessings of peace and the community you give us in Christ.

SC

Friday 16 April

John 20:21–23 (NRSV)

As the Father has sent me, so I send you

Jesus said to them again, 'Peace be with you. As the Father has sent me, so I send you.' When he had said this, he breathed on them and said to them, 'Receive the Holy Spirit. If you forgive the sins of any, they are forgiven them; if you retain the sins of any, they are retained.'

Again Jesus says 'Peace'. Then we hear the words of the great commission: as Jesus has been sent by the Father, who is now their Father, so the disciples are also sent out. They are to go into a despairing world armed only with the joy that can be found through Christ, the peace that Jesus has made between God and humanity and the message of a new creation and a new hope.

How are they to do it—a band of peasant fishermen? They can do it through the Spirit, which is the indwelling presence of Jesus that animates, inspires, provokes and leads.

They are also given authority, the authority that was in Jesus to bring God's reconciliation to the world: 'If you forgive the sins of any, they are forgiven them; if you retain the sins of any, they are retained' (v. 23). The infant Church is given the authority to continue the ministry of Jesus, to bring peace to those who are far off and peace to those who are near, for, through Jesus, all have access to God (Ephesians 2:17–18). This is also our job today. By dwelling deeply in the story of the first Easter, we find ourselves standing in that upper room with the first disciples. We see the risen Lord, hear him speak to us and share the commission given to the disciples.

The joy of Easter dispels the darkness of our own lives and we are given hope and joy. We are inspired to live more joyful and hopeful lives. We begin to see what a reordered world might look like. In Jesus, we see what it *will* look like in the future that awaits us. The peace of Christ is the assurance of our peace with God. It is also the greatest hope for our world.

Prayer

Almighty God, send us out in the power of your Spirit to live and work to your praise and glory.

SC

The deeds of David: 2 Samuel 16—24

These final chapters of 2 Samuel are full of drama: rebellion, betrayal, murder, battles. There are long-haired sons, mighty warriors, schemers, advisers and double agents. Then the book ends with a series of postscripts: a song, a last word, a list of names—and a plague.

We join the story at the point of Absalom's rebellion. David's dysfunctional family is no longer a private embarrassment; the breakdown of the relationship between father and son has become a public liability. For two years they had not spoken to each other. Absalom grasped his chance, usurping his father's popularity and preparing to seize power. David was then forced to leave Jerusalem as civil war loomed.

This is history as a *Boy's Own* adventure story. It is full of action and intrigue. It is certainly not for the faint-hearted or the squeamish, but it is also history that is part of the word of God; it is history with a purpose. This is the inside story of the great king, the 'man after God's own heart' (1 Samuel 13:14), the mighty warrior and the gifted poet. It is the history of the one to whom God had promised that his son's kingdom would be established forever (1 Chronicles 17:11).

The history is uncompromisingly 'warts and all'. The consequences of sin are never more powerfully highlighted and God's redeeming mercy is seen in its glorious fullness. It is a foretaste of what will be accomplished by 'great David's greater Son' (as the hymn puts it) and therefore becomes part of our story.

These chapters are not easy. People's lives are sacrificed for the greater good. David demonstrates that it is one thing to be a celebrity singer-songwriter, but quite another to have to make the hard decisions that come with political power.

We live in an age when politicians are treated with contempt, yet there are more Christian MPs than ever before. How can good people, Spirit-filled people, cope with the temptations and compromises of power? David struggled and the Church has a terrible record of abuse of political and ecclesiastical power.

The answer lies in the paradox that almighty God comes to the weak, the poor and powerless. His Son was apparently defeated by the powers of his day, yet it's the resurrection power of his love that is still transforming the world.

Stephen Rand

2 SAMUEL 16:1–4 (TNIV)

Who can you trust?

There was Ziba, the steward of Mephibosheth, waiting to meet him. He had a string of donkeys saddled and loaded with two hundred loaves of bread, a hundred cakes of raisins, a hundred cakes of figs and a skin of wine. The king asked Ziba, 'Why have you brought these?' Ziba answered, 'The donkeys are for the king's household to ride on, the bread and fruit are for the men to eat, and the wine is to refresh those who become exhausted in the wilderness.' The king then asked, 'Where is your master's grandson?' Ziba said to him, 'He is staying in Jerusalem, because he thinks, "Today the house of Israel will restore to me my grandfather's kingdom."' Then the king said to Ziba, 'All that belonged to Mephibosheth is now yours.'

David is on the run. The breakdown in his relationship with his son Absalom, combined with Absalom's scheming lust for power, have led David to abandon Jerusalem. He has climbed the Mount of Olives weeping and barefoot, full of sorrow and shame. This is perhaps his lowest ebb: majesty marginalised.

Ziba meets him there, offering resources for the retreat. David, perhaps thinking everyone has turned against him, is suspicious. His suspicions, justifiably, increase when he asks the reasons for Ziba's generosity, only to be given an answer so banal in its avoidance of the real question. David probably already knew that donkeys were to ride on and food was to eat!

Ziba had been Saul's steward, instructed by David to look after Mephibosheth, the disabled son of his friend Jonathan, not least by farming his land (2 Samuel 9). So where have these gifts come from? David is so suspicious that he asks after Mephibosheth. Ziba sees his chance and betrays his master. His reward is immediate. David is ready to believe the worst. He has been betrayed by his own son; no doubt the son of his friend is capable of returning kindness with treachery.

I remember being asked to preach in a church that had been badly let down by its pastor. Many felt devastated and bitterly betrayed. It was a painful reminder that, while we must never let our lives be dominated by suspicion, we should never forget that all human beings have the capacity to let us down. Only God can be fully trusted.

Reflection

Do our friends find us trustworthy?

SR

Sunday 18 April

2 SAMUEL 16:5–12 (TNIV, ABRIDGED)

Sticks and stones...

As King David approached Bahurim, a man from the same clan as Saul's family came out from there. His name was Shimei... and he cursed as he came out... 'Get out, get out, you murderer, you scoundrel! The Lord has repaid you for all the blood you shed in the household of Saul, in whose place you have reigned. The Lord has given the kingdom into the hands of your son Absalom. You have come to ruin because you are a murderer!' Then Abishai son of Zeruiah said, 'Why should this dead dog curse my lord the king? Let me go over and cut off his head.'... David then said... 'My son, who is of my own flesh, is trying to take my life. How much more, then, this Benjaminite! Leave him alone; let him curse, for the Lord has told him to. It may be that the Lord will look upon my misery and restore to me his covenant blessing instead of his curse today.'

Yesterday, Ziba came to bless; now Shimei comes to curse. He too had close links with Saul. This is his opportunity for revenge, to rub David's face in his humiliation.

He accuses David of being a murderer because of his treatment of Saul's family. While David's conscience is clear on this account, he must have felt the guilt that stemmed from his treatment of Uriah and Bathsheba (ch. 11). The name-calling is accompanied by stone-throwing (16:6).

Abishai is all for ending the irritation, but David is merciful and curiously accepting of the situation. Perhaps he felt that it was no more than he deserved. He was certainly forced into thinking about where God was in his circumstances of distress.

There are two key things to note. First, he recognised his own responsibility for his situation. Never underestimate how much we continue, as human beings, to follow Adam and Eve's example in the garden of Eden: he blamed her, she blamed the serpent (Genesis 3:12–13). It is hard to accept that a situation may be our fault.

Second, David trusted God to keep his promises, despite his own failings. He looked to him to confirm his 'covenant blessing' rather than be disturbed by Shimei's curses.

Prayer

Loving Father, when we are abused and insulted, help us to keep our focus on you and your loving-kindness. Amen

S

2 Samuel 16:16–21 (TNIV, abridged)

Advisers and advice

Then Hushai the Arkite, David's confidant, went to Absalom and said to him, 'Long live the king!...' Absalom said to Hushai, 'So this is the love you show your friend?...' Hushai said to Absalom, 'No, the one chosen by the Lord, by these people and by all the men of Israel—his I will be... Just as I served your father, so I will serve you.' Absalom said to Ahithophel, 'Give us your advice...' Ahithophel answered, 'Sleep with your father's concubines whom he left to take care of the palace. Then all Israel will hear that you have made yourself obnoxious to your father, and the hands of everyone with you will be more resolute.'

David has left Jerusalem. Absalom moves in, accompanied by Ahithophel, formerly David's trusted adviser. He is greeted by Hushai, another of David's inner group, who stayed behind in Jerusalem at David's request (15:32–34) in order to sow confusion and gather information for David. He loses no time in putting the plan into action.

Absalom is suspicious, but he is also vain, ready to believe his own propaganda. So, when Hushai says 'Long live the king', Absalom is all too ready to assume that Hushai means him rather than David. Hushai's next statement is equally ambiguous, as he promises to serve the one chosen by the Lord and the people. In fact, David was the one known to have been chosen by God, but Hushai promises loyalty to Absalom, who is delighted to see this evidence of his success in taking servants, as well as power, from his father.

Absalom turns first to Ahithophel for advice, however. David had left ten concubines, women from his harem, to look after the palace as he abandoned Jerusalem (15:16). Ahithophel's advice is brutal. By taking these women publicly as his own, women whom he would have inherited on David's death, he would effectively be declaring David as good as dead. Also, Nathan's prophecy after David's adultery would be fulfilled (see 12:11).

Why would this make Absalom's supporters more resolute? Because now there would be no going back. Absalom had usurped his father's position and his supporters could expect no mercy.

Reflection

Women are still sexually abused as a weapon of war and a sign of conquest. Pray for those who live with this stigma across our world.

SR

2 Samuel 17:1–2, 5–7, 10, 14–16 (TNIV, abridged)

The double agent

> Ahithophel said to Absalom, 'I would... set out tonight in pursuit of David. I would attack him while he is weary and weak...' But Absalom said, 'Summon also Hushai the Arkite, so that we can hear what he has to say as well.'... Hushai replied to Absalom, 'The advice Ahithophel has given is not good this time... all Israel knows that your father is a fighter and that those with him are brave...' Absalom and all the men of Israel said, 'The advice of Hushai the Arkite is better than that of Ahithophel.' For the Lord had determined to frustrate the good advice of Ahithophel in order to bring disaster on Absalom. Hushai told Zadok and Abiathar, the priests, '... Now send a message at once and tell David...'

With power secured in the capital, Absalom's advisers turn their attention to the defeat of David and control of the whole country. Ahithophel is clear: a rapid strike is needed. The aim is to kill David and stop a civil war before it can start: 'The death of the man you seek will mean the return of all; all the people will be unharmed' (v. 3).

Absalom and his court are convinced, but Absalom decides to ask Hushai for a second opinion. This is Hushai's chance to make the most of his role as a double agent. He knows that Ahithophel's advice is sound, so how can he persuade Absalom to change his mind?

He decides to exploit David's reputation and play for time. He suggests that finding David will not be easy. Everyone knows that David has years of experience of guerrilla warfare, evading capture and exhausting his pursuers. Hushai argues, ther fore, that Absalom needs the large possible army—and Absalom hi self needs to be at its head.

The appeal to Absalom's pri was successful. He just could n resist the temptation of demo strating that everyone was behi him and leading them to a glorio victory. He wanted to take mo than David's kingdom; he want his reputation as well. Hushai h done his job. The seeds of Absalon downfall had been sown.

Ahithophel knew it, too. He w so devastated by the rejection his advice that he went home a hanged himself (v. 23).

Reflection

When we seek advice, do we listen to those who flatter us or discern what is best?

2 SAMUEL 18:4–14 (TNIV, ABRIDGED)

The end of Absalom

So the king stood beside the gate while all his men marched out... The king commanded Joab, Abishai and Ittai, 'Be gentle with the young man Absalom for my sake.'... Israel's troops were routed by David's men, and the casualties that day were great—twenty thousand men... Now Absalom happened to meet David's men. He was riding his mule, and as the mule went under the thick branches of a large oak, Absalom's hair got caught in the tree. He was left hanging in midair... When one of the men saw what had happened, he told Joab, '... I would not lay a hand on the king's son. In our hearing the king commanded you and Abishai and Ittai, "Protect the young man Absalom for my sake."' Joab said, 'I am not going to wait like this for you.' So he took three javelins in his hand and plunged them into Absalom's heart.

In a story as good as any thriller (17:17–22), David receives Hushai's message and crosses the Jordan, resting in Manahaim and being refreshed with food and drink supplied by welcome allies (vv. 27–29). Absalom then leads his army over the Jordan in pursuit and the stage is set for a decisive battle.

David is persuaded not to lead his army, but as they leave for battle, he gives his men one very clear message: 'Go easy on Absalom.' Absalom was the enemy, the leader of a rebellion, but he was also David's son.

The battle was savage. David's trained troops were better suited to the forest terrain than Absalom's conscripts, who were routed. There were 20,000 casualties, but the most significant was Absalom himself.

Absalom was a handsome man and he was particularly proud of his hair (14:25–26). Now his pride literally caused his downfall (when I was a long-haired teenager back in the 1960s, I remember my mother highlighting this story!). The proud leader had ridden into battle at the head of his army, but then his mount left him to his fate.

The soldier who found him was not willing to risk the wrath of David by disobeying his instructions. Joab had no such qualms. If David was to win the peace, the rebel leader, the focus of the disaffection, had to die.

Reflection

Civil war is bloody, dividing families and devastating nations. Take a moment to pray for countries currently being broken by civil war.

SR

2 SAMUEL 18:33—19:8 (TNIV, ABRIDGED)

A hollow victory

The king was shaken. He went up to the room over the gateway and wept. As he went, he said: 'O my son Absalom! My son, my son Absalom! If only I had died instead of you—O Absalom, my son, my son!' Joab was told, 'The king is weeping and mourning for Absalom.' And for the whole army the victory that day was turned into mourning... The men stole into the city that day as men steal in who are ashamed when they flee from battle... Then Joab... said, '...I see that you would be pleased if Absalom were alive today and all of us were dead. Now go out and encourage your men...' So the king got up and took his seat in the gateway.

Absalom is dead, but when David hears the news, his reaction is extreme: the word translated 'shaken' is the word used for an earthquake. David has now lost three children—and all the deaths can be traced back to the aftershocks of the earthquake David himself caused when he stole Bathsheba from Uriah.

The grief of losing a child is dreadful enough. A parent's bereavement is full of anguish and many can echo that feeling of despair, of wishing they could have been taken instead of their child. How much greater, then, must David's grief have been, knowing that his actions had contributed to his loss? His long estrangement from Absalom and his son's rebellion did not ease the pain, but may even have made it worse. Now there was no chance of reconciliation, or even a final kind word.

Joab still focuses on political realities. Having removed Absalom, he now fears that David will undermine his own army by grieving for the enemy they had risked their lives to fight. His words to David are as hard as his reaction to the opportunity to kill Absalom had been: 'You love those who hate you and hate those who love you' (19:6).

David is persuaded. The grief is suppressed and his men are encouraged as he makes himself available to them. We can imagine, though, that the ache in his heart never went away. He had his kingdom, but the price he paid for it was great. He could now begin his return to Jerusalem, but he would return a sadder man than when he left.

Prayer

Eternal Father, comfort those who mourn, especially those who mourn for a child.

SR

2 SAMUEL 19:15, 18–23 (TNIV, ABRIDGED)

Amnesty

Now the men of Judah had come to Gilgal to go out and meet the king and bring him across the Jordan… They crossed at the ford to take the king's household over and to do whatever he wished. When Shimei son of Gera crossed the Jordan, he fell prostrate before the king and said to him, 'May my lord not hold me guilty. Do not remember how your servant did wrong on the day my lord the king left Jerusalem… For I your servant know that I have sinned…' Then Abishai… said, 'Shouldn't Shimei be put to death for this? He cursed the Lord's anointed.' David replied, 'What does this have to do with you…? Should anyone be put to death in Israel today?…' So the king said to Shimei, 'You shall not die.'

The rebellion was over. It was one thing to win the war, but quite another to win the peace.

As David approaches the Jordan on his triumphant return journey, those who backed the wrong side throw themselves on his mercy. Shimei and Ziba (vv. 17–18) are the first. Shimei knows that it is no good pretending that nothing has happened; his crime will not be forgotten.

Abishai certainly has not forgotten. He was prevented from killing Shimei once; surely now he can exact retribution, can't he? David's reply is the same now as it was before, however, even though the situation is very different. Now the need is for magnanimity. He judges that there is more likelihood of a peaceful future if he shows mercy rather than meting out punishment.

This is a hard road to walk. From Belfast to Soweto, from Berlin to Belgrade, it is never easy to accept that those who have perpetrated atrocities should be allowed an amnesty. The demands of justice may conflict with the desire for peace and a new start. History suggests, however, that mercy and forgiveness may be the only basis on which the seeds of peace can bear fruit.

Mercy and forgiveness are certainly the basis for our own relationship with God. Despite our rebellion, we are welcomed back into the family. Perhaps it was because David had received God's mercy that he was able to extend it to others.

Prayer

Make me a channel of your peace and an agent for reconciliation—in my family, in my community and in your world.

SR

Saturday 24 April

2 SAMUEL 19:24–29 (TNIV, ABRIDGED)

Loyalty

> Mephibosheth, Saul's grandson, also went down to meet the king. He had not taken care of his feet or trimmed his moustache or washed his clothes from the day the king left until the day he returned safely... The king asked him, 'Why didn't you go with me, Mephibosheth?' He said, 'My lord the king, since I your servant am lame, I said, "I will have my donkey saddled and will ride on it, so I can go with the king." But Ziba my servant betrayed me. And he has slandered your servant to my lord the king. My lord the king is like an angel of God; so do whatever you wish...' The king said to him, 'Why say more? I order you and Ziba to divide the land.'

Mephibosheth is the next to face David. He had very publicly declared his loyalty to David by going into mourning the day the king left Jerusalem and remained ceremonially unclean while his exile continued.

He had been betrayed by Ziba. Presumably one of those donkeys that Ziba had brought to David on the day of his departure (16:1) was the very one that Mephibosheth had intended to use to join David, so it had been impossible for him to do so. Once again Mephibosheth is dependent on David's mercy.

David appears to give an abrupt and surprising judgment. The land he had given to Ziba he now insists should be shared between them. It is as if he cannot be bothered to decide between them—or perhaps he feels that he wants to alienate neither Ziba nor Mephibosheth. This is David the magnanimous, David the peacemaker.

There is one other possibility. Is David anticipating Solomon's famous judgment of the two women fighting over a baby (1 Kings 3:16–28)? If so, Mephibosheth passes the test: 'Let him take everything now that my lord the king has returned home safely' (2 Samuel 19:30). Indeed, Mephibosheth seems determined to maintain his loyalty to David. After all, he owes him everything. It may be a simplistic analogy, but God has treated us as David treated Mephibosheth: we have been rescued and brought to eat at the royal table, enjoying the fellowship of the king.

Prayer

Thank you, merciful Father, that you have not treated us as we deserve, but adopted us as children in your family.

SI

Sunday 25 April

2 Samuel 21:1–6 (TNIV, abridged)

Judgment

There was a famine for three successive years; so David sought the face of the Lord. The Lord said, 'It is on account of Saul and his blood-stained house; it is because he put the Gibeonites to death.'… (Now the Gibeonites were not a part of Israel… the Israelites had sworn to spare them, but Saul in his zeal for Israel and Judah had tried to annihilate them.) David asked the Gibeonites, 'What shall I do for you? How shall I make atonement so that you will bless the Lord's inheritance?' The Gibeonites answered him, '… As for the man who destroyed us… let seven of his male descendants be given to us to be killed.'

We have been reading about mercy and magnanimity. Now, suddenly, we are plunged into an episode that seems close to human sacrifice.

This clash of cultures has two aspects, both hard to fathom. The first is that, according to the cultural norms of the day, the Gibeonites had a right to compensation: a solemn promise had been violated (Joshua 9). Broken covenant relationships could only be mended by the shedding of blood. So, seven of Saul's male descendants had to pay for his crime, then the matter would be closed. This seems to us more like the morality of the Mafia than the wisdom of God's chosen king, but the people at that time would have seen this story as demonstrating atonement and mercy.

The second aspect is that there had been a dreadful famine: many more than seven would have died as a result of three years of food shortages. Even now, in our world, a child dies every three seconds as a result of malnutrition. The difference is that we do not ask God what unconfessed sin has caused this daily disaster. Perhaps we should. The silent holocaust of the world's most vulnerable children is neither a regrettable inevitability nor the judgment of God. It is the result of human selfishness, greed and inertia.

David, responsible for the well-being of his people, seeks an explanation from God, and discerns an injustice to be put right. Perhaps we can find some common ground here. When disaster strikes, we should ask God what our responsibility is and act on his answer.

Prayer

Help us to recognise injustice and combat it in your strength and with your loving anger.

SR

Monday 26 April

2 Samuel 22:2–7 (TNIV)

A song of salvation

> 'The Lord is my rock, my fortress and my deliverer; my God is my rock, in whom I take refuge, my shield and the horn of my salvation. He is my stronghold, my refuge and my saviour—from violent people you save me. I called to the Lord, who is worthy of praise, and have been saved from my enemies. The waves of death swirled about me; the torrents of destruction overwhelmed me. The cords of the grave coiled around me; the snares of death confronted me. In my distress I called to the Lord; I called out to my God. From his temple he heard my voice; my cry came to his ears.'

The story is interrupted with a song. We have met David the king, David the mighty warrior; now, once again, we have David the singer-songwriter. The song may not be specific to the events that we have been following each day, but it is certainly not inappropriate at this point.

I never fail to be moved by the fact that we can still sing these songs 3000 years after they were written. Their long-lasting relevance comes from the fact they were born from experience. David didn't write hymns of praise because he had learned the art in a college of music; he wrote them to affirm the reality of God, who was with him day by day.

The words are worth savouring. God is his rock—a point of stability when the world is shaken. God is his fortress—a place of safety and security. God is his saviour—the one who has rescued him from death.

The song is a celebration by someone who has been to the brink of destruction, and returned. That is what makes David's affirmation of God even stronger. He has discovered that, in the darkest hour, the sensible option is to call out to God. Why? Because he always hears our cry.

Of course we should also build our relationship with God when things are going well. God does not simply want to be the fourth emergency service, but his promise is that, when disaster strikes, he will be with us.

Prayer

Thank you, loving Father, that, whatever our circumstances, you are with us. Help us to praise you for who you are and all that you have done for us. Amen

SR

Tuesday 27 April

2 SAMUEL 22:26–31 (TNIV)

Faithful one

'To the faithful you show yourself faithful, to the blameless you show yourself blameless, to the pure you show yourself pure, but to the devious you show yourself shrewd. You save the humble, but your eyes are on the haughty to bring them low. You, Lord, are my lamp; the Lord turns my darkness into light. With your help I can advance against a troop; with my God I can scale a wall. As for God, his way is perfect; the Lord's word is flawless. He shields all who take refuge in him.'

Have you been in a meeting where people are asked to say 'thank you' to God? In my experience, there is often a deafening silence! We do not seem to be very good at verbalising our experience of God. David had no such difficulty. His song goes on, verse after verse, full of joy at all that God has done and is doing and full of praise for all that God is.

God is worthy of our worship because he is faithful. We may let him down; he does not let us down. He is always available, always ready to hear our prayers. We may feel far from God; he is never far from us.

God is worthy of our worship because he brings light. His presence illuminates our world, enabling us to see clearly and walk safely. He is the light that exposes sin and the light that provides life itself.

God is worthy of our worship because he is perfect. Of course, if he was not perfect, he would not be God. That's why the apostle Paul was so amazed: 'God made him who had no sin to be sin for us, so that in him we might become the righteousness of God' (2 Corinthians 5:21). God's perfection is even expressed in his finding the way to bring us into his family.

God is worthy of our worship because he saves. What's more, he saves the humble. He is not dazzled by wealth, but seeks out the weak, inadequate, easily overlooked, ordinary and makes them his children.

Doesn't that make you want to sing?

Reflection

True praise does not require musical talent, just the ability to see God at work. When David thought about God's character and his actions, he was ready to take on the world!

SR

2 SAMUEL 23:1–5 (TNIV, ABRIDGED)

Famous last words

These are the last words of David: '... The Spirit of the Lord spoke through me; his word was on my tongue. The God of Israel spoke, the Rock of Israel said to me: "When one rules over people in righteousness, when he rules in the fear of God, he is like the light of morning at sunrise on a cloudless morning, like the brightness after rain that brings grass from the earth." If my house were not right with God, surely he would not have made with me an everlasting covenant, arranged and secured in every part; surely he would not bring to fruition my salvation and grant me my every desire.'

These may not literally have been David's last words. They were probably more like his final statement, a last will and testament. As he looked back over his extraordinary life and his long relationship with God, he felt confident enough to claim God's authority for his words.

As he anticipated his coming death, not surprisingly, he looked for the positives and held on to the truth at the heart of his experience. The truth was also his hope: God had entered into a covenant with him.

In yesterday's song, David focused on all that God contributed to his people as a result of that covenant relationship. In these last words, he reflects on his own response and responsibility. In a few yet significant words, he defines how a leader under God should be. Ruling in righteousness simply means doing the right thing—in private and in public, treating people fairly in one's personal dealing and ensuring justice in the courts.

A leader chosen by God mus rule in the fear of God. That doe not mean being frightened of th Almighty, but, rather, in every plac and every situation, the king mus remember that he represents Go and his values to the people, tha there is always a higher authorit than himself. Leaders who lead o this basis really can be a blessing t people. Like the sun and the rain they will bring fruitfulness.

What about his very final word David's hope of salvation was base on what God had done. He woul bring it to fruition: that was hi promise.

Prayer

Dear God, in the prime of life and in our final moments, give us the confidence to know that you will keep you promises and grant us your salvation

SI

Thursday 29 April

2 Samuel 23:8–10, 24, 39 (TNIV, abridged)

The mighty warriors

These are the names of David's mighty warriors: Josheb-Basshebeth, a Tahkemonite, was chief of the Three; he raised his spear against eight hundred men, whom he killed in one encounter. Next to him was Eleazar son of Dodai the Ahohite. As one of the three mighty warriors, he was with David when they taunted the Philistines gathered at Pas Dammim for battle. Then the Israelites retreated, but Eleazar stood his ground and struck down the Philistines till his hand grew tired and froze to the sword. The Lord brought about a great victory that day... Among the Thirty were... Uriah the Hittite.

This appendix is a little like the credits that roll up the screen at the end of a film. In the drama that was David's life they were his best 'supporting actors'. 1 Chronicles 11:10 describes them as those who 'gave his kingship strong support'. David may have killed Goliath with no more than a sling and a stone, but the process of establishing his remarkable kingdom involved a tight-knit group of the toughest soldiers.

At the head were 'the Three' (two of whom appear in today's reading) whose deeds were legendary. Josheb-Basshebeth killed 800 men in a single battle; Eleazar fought so hard, his muscles seized up; the third, Shammah, stood his ground when all others had fled and so won a great victory (2 Samuel 23:11–12).

Great leaders need great lieutenants. They know that they cannot do it on their own. David at his best is a role model for Christian leaders. In yesterday's reading, we saw that they should bring blessing to their people by leading in the light of God, their higher authority. Today, we are reminded that effective leadership releases and involves the talents and skills of others.

David at his worst, though, serves as a warning about the temptations of leadership. Under the Three came 'the Thirty'—and last in the list is the name that casts its long shadow over the reign of David: Uriah, the man whose wife and life David stole. The writer has not allowed history to be rewritten and painted him out of the picture. His name is there. We remember the man betrayed by the leader he was prepared to die for, a leader who paid a heavy price for his moral failure.

Reflection

Who is looking to you to stand with them in the battle?

SR

2 SAMUEL 24:18–25 (TNIV, ABRIDGED)

A final legacy

Gad went to David and said to him, 'Go up and build an altar to the Lord on the threshing-floor of Araunah the Jebusite.' So David went up, as the Lord had commanded through Gad… Araunah said, 'Why has my lord the king come to his servant?' 'To buy your threshing-floor,' David answered, 'so I can build an altar to the Lord, that the plague on the people may be stopped.' Araunah said to David, 'Let my lord the king take whatever he wishes and offer it up…' But the king replied to Araunah, 'No, I insist on paying you for it. I will not sacrifice to the Lord my God burnt offerings that cost me nothing.' So David bought the threshing-floor and… built an altar to the Lord there… Then the Lord answered his prayer in behalf of the land, and the plague on Israel was stopped.

The book 2 Samuel ends with a puzzling and awful story. David has made another wrong choice and, in some way, the whole nation is involved and pays the price. God's judgment sees 70,000 men die of the plague. David is full of anguish and seeks God's mercy—hence the visit to Araunah to build an altar.

Araunah is anxious to play his part and donate what is needed, but David is insistent: he will pay. It's a matter of principle: a sacrifice must be a sacrifice. So many Christians long for God's blessing, but the price of obedience can seem too much to pay. The rich young ruler (Luke 18:18–25) was not the last to turn his back on Jesus because the sacrifice was too great.

Gideon had met God on a threshing-floor (Judges 6:37–40) David's ancestors Ruth and Boaz also met each other on a threshing-floor (Ruth 3). On Araunah's threshing-floor, David sought—and found—God's mercy.

In doing so he had, unknowingly, bought the site that would be the place where God dwelled with his people: 'Then Solomon began to build the temple of the Lord in Jerusalem on Mount Moriah… on the threshing-floor of Araunah the Jebusite, the place provided by David' (2 Chronicles 3:1). It was a great return on his investment. Sacrifice is the key to blessing.

Reflection

Love so amazing, so divine,
Demands my soul, my life, my all.

Isaac Watts (1674–1748)

SR

The BRF

Magazine

Richard Fisher writes...

As another new year starts, we at BRF are looking forward to 2010 as well as back at what we have accomplished in the past year. As you will see in my article 'The many sides of BRF', the organisation has developed significantly over the past ten years and the scope of our ministry has expanded dramatically. It has been wonderful to see these changes come into fruition under God's provision for us.

2009 was another busy and productive year. A real highlight was seeing Messy Church go from strength to strength. In February we saw the 100th Messy Church register on the website and, at the time of writing, 145 have signed up, with many more unregistered. Regional coordinators around the UK are helping us to make strong links with individual Messy Churches, and we are seeing many benefits arising from Lucy Moore's full-time focus on developing this ministry as our Messy Church ambassador. It has been a real encouragement to see churches engage with the vision for Messy Church and embrace it as part of their local mission.

We also saw big changes for *Foundations21*, our web-based discipleship resource, in 2009. From May, it was offered as a gift to the church, becoming totally free for anyone to use. This took a huge step of faith for BRF, but we hope that, with the continued support of trusts and churches, as well as the generous donations of *Foundations21* users themselves, we will be able to continue to offer this invaluable resource for some time to come. In this issue of *The BRF Magazine*, Paul Simmonds, *Foundations21* team leader, shares how *Foundations21* has been taken up within Bristol diocese.

Of course, our face-to-face work continues to expand with our *Barnabas* children's ministry in schools and churches, and with our annual Quiet Day programme.

I hope you will enjoy this issue of *The BRF Magazine* and that we may have the opportunity to meet you at one of the many events in which BRF takes part during 2010.

Richard Fisher
Chief Executive

The many sides of BRF

Richard Fisher

Early last year, I talked with a vicar whose church had decided to make BRF one of the charities that they would support financially during 2009. He told me that this had initially come as something of a surprise to him, as he had thought that BRF was mainly a publisher. He had then discovered that there was much more to BRF than just publishing Bible reading notes. Another person, on learning what we actually do, described us as being like an Aladdin's cave, full of hidden treasures. He'd never realised the extent of our ministry today.

For many decades, the primary activity through which BRF fulfilled its charitable purpose was in producing and distributing daily Bible reading notes, along with a number of books, among whose authors were some of the leading Christian writers and communicators of their time.

However, over the past ten years BRF's ministry has evolved significantly into three main areas of activity. Today we still do a lot of publishing, producing about 40 books a year for our BRF and Barnabas imprints, in addition to the three Bible reading notes series, *New Daylight*, *Guidelines* and *Day by Day with God*. (We've just added a fourth, *The Upper Room*, as we have recently become publisher of the UK edition of this international series.) Alongside the publishing we've developed face-to-face ministry, working directly with adults and children in churches and primary schools throughout the country. The internet has come to play an increasingly significant role as well. Our websites enable us to communicate who we are and what we have to offer to resource your spiritual journey; they provide a means for people to purchase our books and Bible reading notes or to book a place to attend a quiet day or training event. The Barnabas in Churches and Barnabas in Schools websites also provide a wealth of ideas and other resources to download and use with children, completely free of charge—something that is widely used and greatly appreciated, judging from the feedback we receive. The Messy Church website enables us to build a sense of community for those developing their own Messy Churches, not just in the UK but increasingly overseas as well, and the *Foundations21* website provides a free, extensive, interactive and flexible learning resource online, so that people can access and use it whenever they want, wherever they happen to be.

This multifaceted approach has opened up many possibilities for us. Whether it's face-to-face, via the web or through printed publications, each aspect of our ministry is complementary to the others. Our books complement the themes of the events and training courses that we run. The Barnabas websites enable us to make available the free ideas and resources that we offer, far beyond the limits of what the team can do face-to-face. The internet has also enabled us to engage directly with many more people than before and to build a sense of fellowship and community with them. This is particularly true, again, for our *Barnabas* children's ministry, where through our regular monthly emails we've been able to offer support, inspiration and encouragement to a growing number of children's leaders and teachers.

Of course, the development of BRF's face-to-face and web-based ministry has created considerable financial challenges. We generate income from the sales of books and Bible reading notes and also from the modest charges that we make for the quiet days and the training events we offer. However, as our ministry has evolved over the last decade in particular, we have needed to secure grant and donor support to fund the new areas of opportunity that have arisen. From having to do very little fundraising ten years ago, it's now a vital aspect of our work.

We have been very humbled by the generosity that has been shown by you, the readers of our Bible reading notes and books, and a number of charitable trusts, as we have shared with you the funding needs and the vision for what we hope to achieve with that support. For example, thanks to your financial support, our Barnabas team has become well-established as a force within children's ministry and its work is highly respected and admired.

Looking back, we've seen a decade of change for BRF, a period in which our core ministries—Bible reading, spirituality, discipleship and working with children under 11—have become established afresh. We need your ongoing support if we're to continue to offer and develop them still further, and our hope is also to encourage more churches to consider supporting BRF as part of their giving to 'home mission'. We need to find ways to make more widely known the hidden treasures in BRF's own 'Aladdin's cave': perhaps this is something you can help us with in your church?

Please turn to page 155 to see how you can help to resource BRF's ministry.

Equipped to grow: *Foundations21* in Bristol Diocese

Paul Simmonds

We arrived in Bristol amid great cheering. It wasn't for Helen and myself but for Bristol Rovers' goal in a match at the ground near where we were staying. I don't know about West Country football but, when it comes to spiritual growth, Bristol Diocese is one to watch. It is not willing to just sit, wait and see what happens to the church in its area; it has committed itself to pray and work proactively for growth.

Bishop Mike Hill and his team of clergy and lay leaders are spear-heading this strategy. To strengthen and encourage the churches, he spoke at three special 'Equipped to grow' Saturday events at which BRF was invited to showcase *Foundations21*. Bristol Diocese was the first area of the country where people experienced *Foundations21* free (or at a subsidised rate) thanks to a generous donation. It was good to meet people who had been using it. We talked to a number of ministers who did not know about the resources for preaching provided in *Foundations21* each week, with links to pages which reflect the lectionary theme for that Sunday.

Bristol is a sausage-shaped diocese, geographically speaking, with over 60 miles between Bristol at one end and Swindon at the other, two of the venues for 'Equipped to grow'. Roughly halfway between them is Chippenham, which was our third venue. There were over 120 people at the Swindon and Chippenham events, and over 300 at Bristol.

A large number of churches sent teams, and we were extremely busy each Saturday, showing people *Foundations21* and offering them a complimentary copy of *Making sense of the Bible*. This latest offering is a stand-alone course based on Room 2, The Bible, in *Foundations21*, reflecting many of the different kinds of learning activities there, including questions, video clips and reflection. It requires a leader who is confident to add their own input and happy with using PowerPoint slides as a way of taking people through the themes. *Making sense of the Bible* is proving to be an excellent introduction to the Bible for newish Christians and a fresh approach for those who have been reading it for longer. It is also a good way of helping people become familiar with the online pages and resources of *Foundations21* because everyone is able to go online after each session and do their own work if they want to. You can find out more about *Making sense of the Bible* on the BRF website.

During these events, Bishop Mike encouraged people to have confidence in their faith and live it out. With the credit crunch affecting so many people, I was struck by the relevance of the section on money in the Lifestyle Room in *Foundations21*, since it not only examines biblical principles on how we spend our money but also has links to pages about debt and how to keep control of spending. Since then, we've added some more links to help people with the issue of redundancy.

Room 12, Mission, is especially relevant to the theme of 'Equipped to grow'. One of the videos there talks about some places in the world where they can't build churches fast enough to accommodate the numbers of people wanting to come together to worship. Another speaks of the need to find new ways of 'being church' and, on their website, Bristol Diocese showcases some of their attempts to do this (www.bristol.anglican.org/ministry/fresh/index.html).

In fact, Bristol Diocese has one of the best diocesan websites, with lots of resources and useful stories. I met Sam Cavender, the man in charge of the website, and discussed with him the value of the internet in Christian ministry. He pointed out some of the ways they have used their website to equip individuals and churches. A good example is their pages on the Diocesan Growth Programme, where there are stories of how people came to faith, including the Bishop's: he leads by example!

Helen and I enjoyed our trips back to the West Country. Many of the churches were known to us from our previous work in the diocese, so it was good to hear how God had led them forward. *Foundations21* is now in the hands of many individuals and church leaders and we pray that it will provide useful resources for discipleship and mission as the diocese continues to grow new Christians.

> *Foundations21* is now available as a gift to the Church, completely free of charge! To order your free registration code, go to:
>
> www.foundations21.org.uk.

Paul Simmonds is Foundations21 Team Leader.

Messy Church

Lucy Moore

Mine has to be the most exciting inbox in the world at the moment. Just this morning I opened it up to find waiting for me an email about a Messy Church happening on the thrillingly named Copper Coast in Australia. There's also one from a Regional Coordinator saying that she's getting a supermarket interested in supporting her five Messy Churches in Cornwall.

Another Regional Coordinator tells me about the 160 people who came to their last Messy Church, and Martyn Payne has mailed to keep me in touch with the rest of the *Barnabas* team and give me invaluable advice, as ever.

Mike Moynagh from the national *Fresh Expressions* team is kindly offering a listening ear, and several conference venues have left details about their facilities as possible venues for an autumn symposium about taking Messy Churches on to maturity. Add to that Radio Solent, who have mailed to ask just how many of our team and children we can fit into their studio to be messy one Sunday morning on air, and an invitation to lead a workshop in Belgium for children's leaders about Messy Church… *in French*, and you'll see why I am one of the few people in the UK to rub her hands in glee as Outlook opens up.

Messy Church is like a large amiable dog that's dragging us along breathlessly on a lead towards... who knows where? It has boundless energy and vitality and seems to know where it's going—a bit like Francis Thompson's 'Hound of heaven' but less scary and, interestingly, very much in front of us. We used to own Pineau, a dog who was so badly trained that she would charge off on a walk without the slightest regard for the person holding the lead. She was fabulous when it snowed and happily hauled sledges laden with small children up and down hills, tongue lolling, but you had to be careful not to be knocked to the ground by her enthusiasm. Messy Church and Pineau have their similarities.

If we play the numbers game, for an idea of how things are galloping along, as I write we have 145 Messy Churches signed up to the Directory on the website (www.messychurch.org.uk), and many more who haven't signed up. Leaders are reporting very wholesome numbers of those belonging to Messy Churches locally. Perhaps 160, as mentioned above, is the highest number I've come across (and most of us would scream and run home if we had to cope with that many), but it's common to have 40, 50 or 60 attending. If you average out at a pessimistic 40 per Messy Church in those 145 registered churches, that's around 5800 people coming to church once a month, many of whom belong to no other church. Feel that tug on the lead: God is using Messy Churches to help more people come to know him.

At Messy Fiestas and similar events to share experiences of Messy Church, there is a huge groundswell of interest and enthusiasm. Seminars at events like the Children's Ministry Conference and the Christian Resources Exhibition are very well attended, with questions and stories bursting unstoppably out of the delegates, and responses afterwards that show how inspired people are to take things further in their own area or parish.

We have to watch our step, though, both with a boisterous hound and with Messy Church. One leader emailed me to say that alongside the joy of seeing growing numbers of children coming with no church background, they are facing problems: 'Volunteers get tired and overloaded and sometimes feel overburdened and we are in danger of losing some... And not enough new ones are coming forward... The key teams are the catering team and the craft team and I think they are both a bit precarious at times.' It would be easy to run out of enthusiasm and become disillusioned and weary. So we're setting up a network of Regional Coordinators across the UK to be a first port of call. Each coordinator will be a fast-response person who offers support when it's needed and finds ways appropriate to the locality to help Messy Church leaders feel part of something bigger, to help them see how their story fits into a wider story of God working all over the country, even all over the world! The website also helps foster a sense of belonging as people share stories, questions, crafts and recipe ideas.

There are so many doors opening up: God is giving us the opportunity to learn from our colleagues in Messy Churches in several different denominations, social contexts and countries about how best to be church among families. Most of all, he's giving us the gift of introducing many people to Jesus who wouldn't otherwise meet him: now *that's* worth being dragged along for!

Lucy Moore works full-time for BRF, promoting Messy Church in the UK and beyond.

Mr Barnabas strikes again

Chris Hudson

'Well, children, that was an exciting assembly from Mr Barnabas, wasn't it?' I inwardly groan, while smiling bravely at the masses of children filling the hall. Mr Barnabas? Who's he? Do I need a bigger name badge? I suppose the deputy head has got it nearly right. There's a lot to take in when a Barnabas team member is running a day of RE workshops and an assembly in your school, your head teacher's been called away on an emergency, and you've got to say something to the nice man with a guitar who's just had hundreds of children hand-jiving to a souped-up version of 'The wise man built his house upon the rock'.

Barnabas RE Days are always a little unpredictable. A school asks for a day's workshops on a set theme ('Who am I?', 'Who is my neighbour?' among others) and the team member turns up at the school on the day with props, books and a slight apprehension about what might happen in the next few hours. Of course, we have prepared scripts, a whole series of tried-and-tested routines designed to draw children into thinking about Bible stories and Christian ideas in a new way. There'll be drama, storytelling, games and, in my case, a little music too. Each Barnabas team member brings their own talents to the presentation, and mine often involve a guitar. Children like guitars, you know. And harmonicas.

Regardless of all our preparation, though, we're never quite sure what's going to happen. I've been suddenly asked to add an extra storytelling session just for the Reception class (quick, grab a cuddly toy!) or stretch a session designed for 30 children into one to fit 60 (never mind the quality). A sudden opportunity may present itself. So let's see, we're going to finish the day with a Christingle service in church? Then let's have all the children in the service performing one of the pieces we've worked on together in our class workshops. So they do, and their adoring parents are suitably proud.

But what do the children get out of it? Judging from their responses, they grasp an opportunity to think differently about spiritual stories such as the parable of the good Samaritan. Why should someone stop to help a stranger? And what motivated the most unlikely man of all to stop and help? In a 'conscience alley' exercise, children make their own suggestions: 'He might be you'; 'He might help you one day'; 'Could you live with yourself if you didn't stop?' Of course, there are also reasons just to keep on walking by on the other side: 'You might catch what he's got'; 'He's your enemy'; 'You're in a hurry!' It's all about rediscovering the choices and dilemmas that life presents to us and trying to find the right thing to do—the godly thing that's often not as obvious as we'd like to think.

On one occasion, when exploring the story of Jesus and the leper, we first tried to understand the mindset of a society that blames people for being sick because they're obviously being 'punished' by God—and then imagined how it might feel to be caught in that situation, totally cut off from one's community through fear and prejudice. 'I'd feel angry,' said one child. 'Lonely,' said another. 'They're treating me like a monster!' said a third, picturing himself in the role.

Then, Jesus doesn't just promise to heal the man—he touches him, too. How would you feel if that was you? 'I'd be afraid he was going to catch it too,' said one child. 'I wouldn't believe it was happening,' suggests someone else. 'I'd be amazed that anyone was touching me after all this time,' chips in another. This simple story of Jesus' compassion is incredibly powerful when explored imaginatively, from the inside. All of a sudden, we're entering the story for ourselves, feeling its humanity and wondering how we might respond as well.

Of course, none of this is rocket science for a trained teacher, but you have to know your material, be comfortable with it and have some sensitive responses ready for when children begin opening up. Teaching staff appreciate having another professional coming into school to work with their class, as it gives them the chance to observe their own pupils at work with someone else—a rare luxury.

It also helps that the children do no reading or writing, as pupils with special needs can make a full contribution without worrying about 'getting it wrong'—again. In fact, some of the most interesting verbal and non-verbal responses are often volunteered by children with behavioural difficulties, because they recognise that there is something here for them, that welcomes their contribution and treats them with respect.

So, if that's one effect of my becoming 'Mr Barnabas' for a day—I'll take it!

Chris Hudson is a member of the Barnabas team, based in the north-east of England.

The Editor recommends...

Naomi Starkey

As we enter the early days of January, most of us will be making some kind of New Year resolutions for the months ahead. For many, this will involve vowing (as we probably do every year) to take more exercise, spend quality time with the family, try a different holiday destination, take up a new hobby and so on.

In all this planning and vowing, it can be easy to forget the whole area of Christian discipleship, however. We may be quick to consider taking out a gym membership but slower to think about finding more time to pray each day, to study the Bible more closely or read a book to help us with a difficult theological issue.

Two books recently published by BRF can help readers in very different ways to build up their faith-related knowledge. One is pure fun at first glance but has the interesting side-effect of boosting Bible knowledge, almost without the reader being aware of it. The other is a systematic and user-friendly introduction to a key area of Christian understanding.

Quick Bible Crosswords is BRF's second book of Bible-linked puzzles, following the success of *Three Down, Nine Across* by John Capon. Among the more demanding clues from the 80 non-cryptic crosswords are to name (in eight letters) a coastal town to the north-west of Jerusalem; to identify the chamberlain of Ahasuerus in Esther 1 (six letters) and to remember what the eighth commandment forbids us to do (five letters).

A further challenge is that the clues are all based on the King James Version of the Bible, a translation that will be familiar to many older readers but that quite possibly remains an undiscovered treasure for those brought up in the era of the NIV and *The Message*.

First published in *The Church of England Newspaper*, these crosswords are an entertaining way to check out how well we know the ins and outs of the Bible, as well as our general knowledge. They are compiled by Derek Banes, who has been preparing puzzles for the newspaper since 1998. After more than 30 years as an engineer for the Marconi Company, he took early retirement and started spending more time puzzle-setting and solving.

The Apostles' Creed may well feature as a clue in *Quick Bible Crosswords* (having edited my way through every one of the 80 puzzles, I suppose I ought to remember!), but for in-depth learning about this ancient piece of Christian doctrine, BRF's 'user's guide' to the creed is an invaluable resource.

We may or may not belong to a church that regularly recites the Apostles' Creed as part of Sunday worship, but we are probably familiar with at least some of its cadences: 'I believe in God, the Father almighty, creator of heaven and earth...' In its majestic opening phrases, we can sense the passion of the early Church to define and substantiate the core of Christian belief.

In the face of numerous heresies in the turbulent first centuries of the Church's life, the Apostles' Creed was written to declare the uniqueness of the three-in-one God, as well as setting out the universal scope of the divine work of salvation.

Simply entitled *The Apostles' Creed*, this BRF book is an accessible introduction to what remains the most widely used of all Christendom's confessions of faith. Going through each phrase in turn, author Marshall D. Johnson unpacks the creed's meaning and explains its significance both in historical terms and for Christians today. While the creed does not, of course, spell out how we are to live as disciples in today's world, it remains an enduring and unique 'rule of faith' that provides continuity of belief from past generations into our own time.

In writing the book, Marshall D. Johnson draws on years of experience as a biblical scholar, Lutheran pastor and editorial director of Fortress Press, USA. He has written several other books, including *Psalms through the Year: spiritual exercises for every day* (Augsburg, 2006) and *The Evolution of Christianity: twelve crises that shaped the Church* (Continuum, 2005).

Only the unfolding of the year will reveal whether we stuck to our vow to help out at home more, get properly fit or start learning Japanese. Taking time to nurture our spiritual health may or may not produce rapid results but the long-term benefits are immeasurable and we will probably find that much else in life falls naturally into place as well. Getting to know the Bible better; getting to understand what we believe and why—two resolutions that are definitely worth making and keeping.

And what about the answers to those three clues? Well, you'll just have to get hold of a copy of the book and turn to the back to find out!

To order a copy of any of the BRF books mentioned above, please turn to the order form on page 159.

An extract from *Giving It Up*

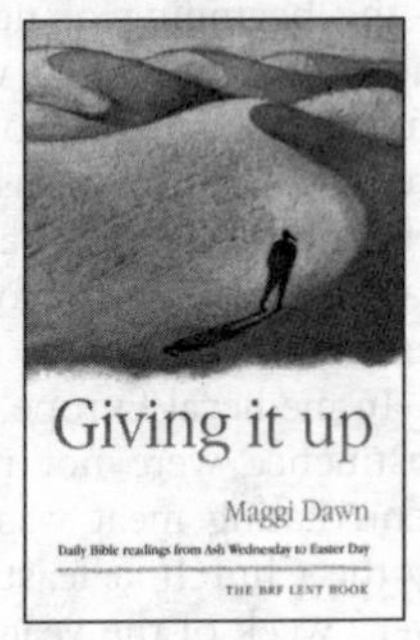

The idea of 'giving something up for Lent' is widely known—yet how many of us simply abstain from some treat or other for a few weeks and fail to engage with the deeper meaning of Lent? BRF's Lent book for 2010, by Maggi Dawn, shows how this can be a time to explore a different kind of 'giving up', one that can transform our lives. If we allow the Holy Spirit to shed his light on our ideas of God that are too harsh, too small, too fragile or too stern, then God will bring us to a profound Easter joy. The extract below is the Introduction to the book.

Introduction

The real voyage of discovery consists not in seeking new landscapes but in having new eyes.
MARCEL PROUST

Of all the traditions associated with Lent, probably the best-known is the practice of giving something up for the six and a half weeks from Ash Wednesday to Easter Sunday. The most common things people give up are chocolate, alcohol, coffee and sweets. Some people give up something non-edible—a time-consuming habit, for instance, like watching TV or surfing the net—and some take the opportunity of Lent to kick a habit like smoking or swearing. But why do we give things up? Where did the tradition begin, and what is it supposed to achieve?

There's clear evidence that for at least 1500 years the Church has kept a period of fasting during the weeks leading up to Easter, and it's thought that it may date even further back to the very early Church. The word 'Lent' comes from the Anglo-Saxon word *Lencten*, from which we get our word 'lengthen', and it referred simply to the fact that the weeks leading up to Easter were the early spring days that were lengthening after the winter solstice. The oldest traditions of Lent are interwoven with the idea of spring. Greek Orthodox communities treat the first day of Lent as a celebration of the first outdoor day of the new year: spring is the beginning of new life after the death that came with winter, and so we should go outside to greet it. All these ideas, of course, reflect the fact that the old Lenten traditions were developed in the northern hemisphere.

In medieval Europe, fasting and abstinence were not restricted to Lent. Eating meat was prohibited by the Church at least one day in every week of the year, and Friday continued to be a 'fish day' until late into the 20th century, as a reminder that it was on Friday that Christ died. In addition to Friday, there were often two or three more days of abstinence in the week, with a great deal of local variation. For instance, in some areas Wednesday was a meat-free day to remember the treason of Judas Iscariot; Saturday was a day to honour the Virgin Mary. There was also a cycle of fasting through the year—the four Ember Days, which mark the beginning of the new seasons, and Advent (the four weeks before Christmas) as well as Lent. So, for the medieval Christian, meat was prohibited for somewhere between a third and a half of all the days in the year; but the Lent fast, representing the 40 days during which Jesus withdrew into the wilderness, was the toughest.

This fast has several purposes. It's supposed to remind us daily that we depend upon God for everything, to draw us closer to God in prayer, to reconnect us to the idea of community, and to help us follow Christ's journey through the wilderness and on to Jerusalem. It's all too easy, though, simply to give up some treat or other for the duration of Lent, feel pleased with ourselves for breaking a bad habit or losing a little weight (or feel a little guilty at not keeping our resolution!) and not really engage with the deeper meaning of Lent.

In the Old Testament, the prophets called the people of God to a 'true fast', one that was not merely the observance of traditions but one that transformed their lives. As we walk through Lent this year, we can explore the idea that there is another kind of 'giving up' that we could do. If we're to draw closer to God, we need to be willing to give up some of our entrenched ideas about God in order to see him more clearly. It's not so much giving up 'false gods'; it's more about identifying false or blurred images of God that have been picked up from the surrounding culture or from our imagination, and allowing them to be replaced. We need to allow the light to be shed on those places where our idea of God is too harsh, too weak, too small, too fragile, too stern.

We'll begin this Lent journey,

then, by looking at the traditions of Lent to gain a clearer picture of what they are for, and what biblical imagery they reflect. Then we'll see what Jesus said about fasting and what he gave up when he fasted in the wilderness. We'll look at the way some Old Testament characters traded in their old idea of God for a true encounter, and see how different the real God was from their expectations. Then we'll see how Jesus turned people's ideas about God upside down. Finally, in Holy Week we'll follow some of the events of the last week in Jesus' life, and discover how different he was from the Messiah people were expecting. In the process, we may find that our own preconceived notions of what God 'ought' to be like come in for some re-examination.

This Lent, then, whether or not you're giving up chocolate or anything else, I invite you to take a journey with me through biblical tales of fasts and wildernesses to seek a clearer vision of God. As we travel, let's pray for grace to be flexible enough in our thinking to give up entrenched ideas and allow God to reveal himself to us. As I've been writing this book, I've been surprised at the way in which my own ideas have been changed all over again. To see God more clearly almost certainly means being surprised at what we discover.

Let's take the prayer of St Richard of Chichester (1197–1253) as our daily prayer:

Thanks be to thee,
my Lord Jesus Christ,
For all the benefits
thou hast won for me,
For all the pains and insults
thou hast borne for me.
O most merciful Redeemer,
Friend, and Brother,
May I know thee more clearly,
Love thee more dearly,
And follow thee more nearly,
Day by day.

Maggi Dawn is an Anglican priest, currently Chaplain and Fellow of Robinson College, University of Cambridge, where she teaches theology. She has written several hymns and worship songs and has contributed to Guidelines. *She has her own website: http://maggidawn.typepad.com/maggidawn and she is also the author of* Beginnings and Endings, *the BRF Advent book for 2007.*

To order a copy of Giving It Up, *please turn to the order form on page 159.*

New Daylight © BRF 2010

The Bible Reading Fellowship
15 The Chambers, Vineyard, Abingdon OX14 3FE
Tel: 01865 319700; Fax: 01865 319701
E-mail: enquiries@brf.org.uk; Website: www.brf.org.uk

ISBN 978 1 84101 548 4

Distributed in Australia by:
Willow Connection, PO Box 288, Brookvale, NSW 2100.
Tel: 02 9948 3957; Fax: 02 9948 8153;
E-mail: info@willowconnection.com.au
Available also from all good Christian bookshops in Australia.
For individual and group subscriptions in Australia:
Mrs Rosemary Morrall, PO Box W35, Wanniassa, ACT 2903.

Distributed in New Zealand by:
Scripture Union Wholesale, PO Box 760, Wellington
Tel: 04 385 0421; Fax: 04 384 3990; E-mail: suwholesale@clear.net.nz

Distributed in Canada by:
The Anglican Book Centre, 80 Hayden Street, Toronto, Ontario, M4Y 3G2
Tel: 001 416 924-1332; Fax: 001 416 924-2760;
E-mail: abc@anglicanbookcentre.com; Website: www.anglicanbookcentre.com

Publications distributed to more than 60 countries

Acknowledgments

The New Revised Standard Version of the Bible, Anglicized Edition, copyright © 1989, 1995 by the Division of Christian Education of the National Council of the Churches of Christ in the USA. Used by permission. All rights reserved.

The Holy Bible, New International Version, copyright © 1973, 1978, 1984, 1995 by International Bible Society. Used by permission of Hodder & Stoughton Publishers, a division of Hodder Headline Ltd. All rights reserved. 'NIV' is a registered trademark of International Bible Society. UK trademark number 1448790.

The Holy Bible, Today's New International Version, copyright © 2004 by International Bible Society. Used by permission of Hodder & Stoughton Publishers, a division of Hodder Headline Ltd. All rights reserved. 'TNIV' is a registered trademark of International Bible Society.

The New Jerusalem Bible published and copyright © 1985 by Darton, Longman and Todd Ltd and les Editions du Cerf, and by Doubleday, a division of Bantam Doubleday Dell Publishing Group, Inc. Used by permission of Darton, Longman and Todd Ltd, and Doubleday, a division of Random House, Inc.

The Good News Bible published by The Bible Societies/HarperCollins Publishers Ltd, UK © American Bible Society 1966, 1971, 1976, 1992, used by permission.

The Holy Bible, New Living Translation copyright © 1996, 2004. Used by permission of Tyndale House Publishers, Inc., Wheaton, Illinois 60189. All rights reserved.

Extracts from the Authorised Version of the Bible (The King James Bible), the rights in which are vested in the Crown, are reproduced by permission of the Crown's Patentee, Cambridge University Press.

Printed in Singapore by Craft Print International Ltd

SUPPORTING BRF'S MINISTRY

As a Christian charity, BRF is involved in five distinct yet complementary areas. Through our **BRF** ministry (www.brf.org.uk), we're resourcing adults for their spiritual journey through Bible reading notes, books, and a programme of quiet days and teaching days. BRF also provides the infrastructure that supports our other four specialist ministries.

Our **Foundations21** ministry (www.foundations21.org.uk) is providing flexible and innovative ways for individuals and groups to explore their Christian faith and discipleship through a multimedia internet-based resource.

Led by Lucy Moore, our **Messy Church** ministry is enabling churches all over the UK (and increasingly abroad) to reach children and adults beyond the fringes of the church (visit www.messychurch.org.uk).

Through our **Barnabas in Churches** ministry, we're helping churches to support, resource and develop their children's ministry with the under-11s more effectively (visit www.barnabasinchurches.org.uk).

Our **Barnabas in Schools** ministry (www.barnabasinschools.org.uk) is enabling primary school children and teachers to explore Christianity creatively and bring the Bible alive within RE and Collective Worship.

At the heart of BRF's ministry is a desire to equip adults and children for Christian living—helping them to read and understand the Bible, to explore prayer and to grow as disciples of Jesus. In an increasingly secular world, people need this help more than ever. We can do something about it, but our resources are limited. We need your help to make a real impact on the local church, local schools and the wider community.

- You could support BRF's ministry with a donation or standing order (using the response form overleaf).
- You could consider making a bequest to BRF in your will. (We have a leaflet available with more information about this, which can be requested using the form overleaf.)
- You could encourage your church to support BRF as part of your church's giving to home mission—perhaps focusing on a specific area of our ministry, or a particular member of our Barnabas team.
- Most important of all, you could support BRF with your prayers.

If you would like to discuss how a specific gift or bequest could be used in the development of our ministry, Chief Executive Richard Fisher would be delighted to talk further with you, either on the telephone or in person. Please let us know if you would like him to contact you.

Whatever you can do or give, we thank you for your support.

BRF MINISTRY APPEAL RESPONSE FORM

Name ____

Address ____

____ Postcode ________

Telephone ____________________ Email ____________________

(tick as appropriate)

Gift Aid Declaration

❑ I am a UK taxpayer. I want BRF to treat as Gift Aid Donations all donations I make from 6 April 2000 until I notify you otherwise.

Signature ________________________________ Date __________

❑ I would like to support BRF's ministry with a regular donation by standing order (please complete the Banker's Order below).

Standing Order – Banker's Order

To the Manager, Name of Bank/Building Society

Address ____

____ Postcode ________

Sort Code ____________________ Account Name ____________________

Account No ____

Please pay Royal Bank of Scotland plc, Drummonds, 49 Charing Cross, London SW1A 2DX (Sort Code 16-00-38), for the account of BRF A/C No. 00774151

The sum of ______ pounds on ___ / ___ / ___ (insert date your standing order starts) and thereafter the same amount on the same day of each month until further notice.

Signature ________________________________ Date __________

Single donation

❑ I enclose my cheque/credit card/Switch card details for a donation of £5 £10 £25 £50 £100 £250 (other) £ ______ to support BRF's ministry

Credit/Switch card no. ☐☐☐☐☐☐☐☐☐☐☐☐☐☐☐☐

Expires ☐☐☐☐ **Security code** ☐☐☐ **Issue no. (Switch card only)** ☐☐☐☐

Signature ________________________________ Date __________

(Where appropriate, on receipt of your donation, we will send you a Gift Aid form)

❑ Please send me information about making a bequest to BRF in my will.

Please detach and send this completed form to: Richard Fisher, BRF, 15 The Chambers, Vineyard, Abingdon OX14 3FE. BRF is a Registered Charity (No.233280)

NEW DAYLIGHT SUBSCRIPTIONS

Please note our subscription rates 2010–2011. From the May 2010 issue, the new subscription rates will be:

Individual subscriptions covering 3 issues for under 5 copies, payable in advance (including postage and packing):

	UK	SURFACE	AIRMAIL
NEW DAYLIGHT each set of 3 p.a.	£14.40	£15.90	£19.20
NEW DAYLIGHT 3-year sub i.e. 9 issues	£36.00	N/A	N/A
(Not available for Deluxe)			
NEW DAYLIGHT DELUXE each set of 3 p.a.	£18.00	£22.50	£28.80

Group subscriptions covering 3 issues for 5 copies or more, sent to ONE address (post free):

NEW DAYLIGHT	£11.40	each set of 3 p.a.
NEW DAYLIGHT DELUXE	£14.97	each set of 3 p.a.

Please note that the annual billing period for Group Subscriptions runs from 1 May to 30 April.

Copies of the notes may also be obtained from Christian bookshops:

NEW DAYLIGHT	£3.80 each copy
NEW DAYLIGHT DELUXE	£4.99 each copy

SUBSCRIPTIONS

❑ Please send me a Bible reading resources pack
❑ I would like to take out a subscription myself (complete your name and address details only once)
❑ I would like to give a gift subscription (please complete both name and address sections below)

Your name ____________________
Your address ____________________
____________________ Postcode ________
Tel ____________ Email ____________________

Gift subscription name ____________________
Gift subscription address ____________________
____________________ Postcode ________

Gift message (20 words max.) ____________________
____

Please send *New Daylight* beginning with the May / September 2010 / January 2011 issue: (delete as applicable)

(please tick box)	UK	SURFACE	AIR MAIL
NEW DAYLIGHT	❑ £14.40	❑ £15.90	❑ £19.20
NEW DAYLIGHT 3-year sub	❑ £36.00		
NEW DAYLIGHT DELUXE	❑ £18.00	❑ £22.50	❑ £28.80
NEW DAYLIGHT daily email only	❑ £12.00 (UK and overseas)		
NEW DAYLIGHT email + printed	❑ £23.40	❑ £24.90	❑ £28.20

Confirm your email address ____________________

Please complete the payment details below and send, with appropriate payment, to: **BRF, 15 The Chambers, Vineyard, Abingdon OX14 3FE.**

Total enclosed £ ________ (cheques should be made payable to 'BRF')

Please charge my Visa ❑ Mastercard ❑ Switch card ❑ with £ ________

Card number ☐☐☐☐☐☐☐☐☐☐☐☐☐☐☐☐

Expires ☐☐☐☐ **Security code** ☐☐☐ **Issue no (Switch only)** ☐☐☐☐

Signature (essential if paying by credit/Switch) ____________________

BRF is a Registered Charity

BRF PUBLICATIONS ORDER FORM

Please ensure that you complete and send off both sides of this order form.

Please send me the following book(s):		Quantity	Price	Total
680 1	Giving It Up *(M. Dawn)*	____	£7.99	____
569 9	Fasting and Feasting *(G. Giles)*	____	£7.99	____
3256 9	A Feast for Lent *(D. Smith)*	____	£6.99	____
587 3	Into Your Hands *(K. Scully)*	____	£5.99	____
596 5	The Road to Easter Day *(J. Godfrey)*	____	£5.99	____
538 5	My First Easter Sticker Book *(S.A. Wright)*	____	£3.50	____
707 5	The Barnabas Classic Children's Bible *(R. Davies)*	____	£11.99	____
526 2	The Barnabas Children's Bible *(R. Davies)*	____	£12.99	____
530 9	My First Bible *(L. Lane)*	____	£6.99	____
712 9	Quick Bible Crosswords *(D. Banes)*	____	£6.99	____
547 7	Three Down, Nine Across *(J. Capon)*	____	£6.99	____
679 5	The Apostles' Creed *(M.D. Johnson)*	____	£5.99	____
503 3	Messy Church *(L. Moore)*	____	£8.99	____
602 3	Messy Church 2 *(L. Moore)*	____	£8.99	____
528 6	Six Men Encountering God *(B. Lincoln)*	____	£6.99	____
066 3	PBC: Exodus *(H.R. Page Jnr)*	____	£8.99	____
030 4	PBC: 1&2 Samuel *(H. Mowvley)*	____	£7.99	____
029 8	PBC: John *(R.A. Burridge)*	____	£8.99	____
012 0	PBC: Galatians and 1 & 2 Thessalonians *(J. Fenton)*	____	£7.99	____

Total cost of books £ ________

Donation £ ________

Postage and packing £ ________

TOTAL £ ________

POSTAGE AND PACKING CHARGES				
order value	UK	Europe	Surface	Air Mail
£7.00 & under	£1.25	£3.00	£3.50	£5.50
£7.01–£30.00	£2.25	£5.50	£6.50	£10.00
Over £30.00	free	prices on request		

See over for payment details.

All prices are correct at time of going to press, are subject to the prevailing rate of VAT and may be subject to change without prior warning.

PAYMENT DETAILS

Please complete the payment details below and send with appropriate payment and completed order form to:

BRF, 15 The Chambers, Vineyard,
Abingdon OX14 3FE

Name ______________________________

Address ______________________________

______________________________ Postcode ______________

Telephone ______________________________

Email ______________________________

Total enclosed £ ____________ (cheques should be made payable to 'BRF')

Please charge my Visa ❑ Mastercard ❑ Switch card ❑ with £ ________

Card number: ☐☐☐☐☐☐☐☐☐☐☐☐☐☐☐☐

Expires: ☐☐☐☐ Security code ☐☐☐ Issue no (Switch only): ☐☐☐

Signature (essential if paying by credit/Switch) ______________________

❑ Please do not send me further information about BRF publications.

ALTERNATIVE WAYS TO ORDER

Christian bookshops: All good Christian bookshops stock BRF publications. For your nearest stockist, please contact BRF.

Telephone: The BRF office is open between 09.15 and 17.30. To place your order, phone 01865 319700; fax 01865 319701.

Web: Visit www.brf.org.uk

BRF is a Registered Charity